Praise for *Teach Your Team to Fish*

"*Teach Your Team to Fish* is filled with powerful insights drawn from the life of Jesus. Delving into the riches of his leadership wisdom, Laurie Beth Jones offers fresh perspective and provocative challenges that will equip leaders to propel their teams toward innovation and excellence."

–Wayne Hastings, coauthor of
*Trust Me: Developing a Leadership
Style People Will Follow*

"Think of it. Whoever built a higher performing team than Jesus! Now Laurie Beth Jones makes this ancient wisdom accessible and useful to twenty-first-century leaders. Learn from the Master."

–Bob Buford, author of
*Halftime: Changing Your Game Plan
from Success to Significance* and
*Stuck in Halftime: Reinvesting
Your One and Only Life*

"Laurie Beth Jones beautifully points aspiring team leaders and builders to the Master Servant Leader and Builder, Jesus Christ. *Teach Your Team to Fish* is rich in inspiration and instruction . . . well worth the read, and can be life-changing."

–Commissioner Robert A. Watson,
retired national commander,
Salvation Army, and author of
The Most Effective Organization in the U.S.

"*Teach Your Team to Fish* has all the ingredients of a terrific book. Laurie Beth Jones has shared her expertise on the subject of team building with a cutting edge focus on marketplace words like *community* and *connection*."

–Stan Toler, author of *The Secret Blend*

Praise for *Jesus, CEO*

"A perfect book for leaders looking to model a kind and loving leadership style. Jones gives you many practical ideas on how to add love, inspiration, and goodwill into your organization."

— Ken Blanchard, coauthor of *The One Minute Manager*

"I was deeply impacted as I read this book . . . Laurie Beth Jones has put together a powerful book that will influence corporate America."

— Pat Williams, general manager, Orlando Magic

"[Laurie Beth Jones is] on the leading edge of the spiritual and business movement in this country. . . . [*Jesus, CEO*] is a phenomenal blend of practical wisdom and spiritual truths that is humorous, profound, and highly readable."

— George Marks, director, Red Rose Distribution

"Jones presents Jesus not as a religious messiah but as an executive leader . . . A kind of how-to manual for succeeding as corporate officers — internally, externally, and for eternity."

— *San Diego Union Tribune*

"[Jones'] sentiments as expressed here ring with sincerity. Her thoughtful use of Jesus' biblical sayings on belief, boldness, discipline, and the like add to her credibility."

— *Publishers Weekly*

"This book's strength lies in its ability to surprise two very different groups of readers: those put off by a title slanted toward corporate success and those attracted by the title's promise of a step-by-step guide to such success . . . Practical and pithy advice for anyone (whether CEO or not) who works with other people to get things done."

— *Booklist*

The Path

"Laurie Beth Jones sprinkles the narrative with enough humor and personal detail that it's easy to be swept along . . . It's the blend of the fabulous and the personal that makes *The Path* so inspirational. Readers who identify with Jones's Christianity will find the book transcendent; those who don't will still be pulled along to examine their talents, values, and purpose."

— *Worldbusiness*

"Offer[s] practical, useful help to Christians and nonbelievers alike. Jones has made her mark, and her books are here to stay."

— *Christian Retailing*

The Power of Positive Prophecy

"I'm a Laurie Beth Jones fan. Her book *The Power of Positive Prophecy* offers a unique perspective on prophecy. Read it! Laurie Beth cares about you and wants to help you make the most of your life."

— Ken Blanchard, coauthor of *The One Minute Manager*

Praise for Laurie Beth Jones

"[Jones's] style is engaging and breezy with enough personal details and humor that make it easy to be swept along. While loosely hitting biblical touchstones, she makes an embracing case for Jesus as a modern role model."

— Tom Depoto, *Star-Ledger* (Newark, N.J.)

Also by Laurie Beth Jones

Jesus, CEO
Using Ancient Wisdom for Visionary Leadership

The Path
Creating Your Mission Statement for Work and for Life

Jesus in Blue Jeans
A Practical Guide to Everyday Spirituality

Grow Something Besides Old
Seeds for a Joyful Life

The Power of Positive Prophecy
Finding the Hidden Potential in Everyday Life

Jesus, Inc.:
The Visionary Path
An Entrepreneur's Guide to True Success

TEACH
YOUR TEAM
TO FISH

Using Ancient Wisdom
for Inspired Teamwork

LAURIE BETH JONES

Foreword by Ken Blanchard

WATERBROOK
PRESS

Published by Three Rivers Press, New York, New York.
Member of the Crown Publishing Group, a division of Random House, Inc.
www.crownpublishing.com

This book is copublished with WaterBrook Press, 2375 Telstar Drive, Suite 160,
Colorado Springs, Colorado 80920, a division of Random House, Inc.

Three Rivers Press and the Tugboat design are registered
trademarks of Random House, Inc.

WaterBrook and its deer design logo are registered trademarks of
WaterBrook Press, a division of Random House, Inc.

Originally published in hardcover by Crown Business,
a division of Random House, Inc., in 2002.

Printed in the United States of America

Design by Leonard W. Henderson

Library of Congress Cataloging-in-Publication Data
Jones, Laurie Beth.
Teach your team to fish : using ancient wisdom for inspired teamwork /
Laurie Beth Jones.
Includes index.
1. Teams in the workplace.   2. Executive ability.   3. Leadership.   4. Jesus
Christ—Leadership.   I. Title
HD66 .J655 2002
658.4'02—dc21   2001047743

ISBN 1-4000-5311-0 (Crown)
ISBN 1-57856-977-X (WaterBrook)

10 9 8 7 6 5 4 3 2 1

First Paperback Edition

To Doug Hawthorne, one of the greatest Fishermen I have ever met, and to all teambuilders everywhere, who stand on the shore and feel humbled by just how deep the sea really is.

CONTENTS

FOREWORD

Today, as never before in history, organizational leaders are realizing that to maximize performance people need to be organized in teams. No longer can we depend upon a few peak performers to make the difference. The mantra today is "none of us is as smart as all of us."

People who "get" the importance of teamwork and are breaking new ground in the area of teambuilding, often think of themselves as creative innovators. That's what I used to think I was years ago when I helped develop Situation Leadership® and *The One Minute Manager*® —both considered groundbreaking management concepts. That was all before I began to study Jesus as a leader. I soon discovered that everything I ever wrote about or taught Jesus did. All I was doing was rediscovering what He had already proven as simple truths about working with people.

How was that possible? Easy! After all, Jesus was the greatest leader of all time. Regardless of your religious persuasion, you have to admit that Jesus was an incredible leader. He hired twelve incompetent guys. None of His disciples had any experience in becoming "fishers of men." The only one with any real education was Judas, and he was Jesus' only turnover problem. And yet, with this diverse, seemingly ragtag group, Jesus changed the world forever.

So is there any surprise that Jesus knew that He could not

effectively do His work on earth without the benefit of a team? Nor that He knew how to build a High Five! team better than Phil Jackson or Joe Torre ever dreamed of doing? For me there was little surprise. That's why I love *Teach Your Team to Fish: Using Ancient Wisdom to Inspire Teamwork.* It's one of the best teambuilding books I've ever read.

Laurie Beth Jones does it again. She draws out of Jesus' ministry wisdom that can help all of us be better teambuilders, whether we are parents, corporation presidents, leaders of nonprofit organizations, coaches, teachers, or volunteer leaders. She said it well: "Jesus came not to give us platitudes and promises, but to teach us how to fish—how to pull together like the fishermen hauling in their nets" and gathering "a catch that [became] legendary."

Reading this book will prepare you to be a team leader that excites, grounds, transforms, and releases your people to perform at higher levels than you or they ever dreamed possible. Thanks, Laurie Beth, for proving once again that Jesus is the greatest leader of all time, and He wants to be *our teacher.* May we always remember, "If God be for us, who can be against us?" God bless.

Ken Blanchard
coauthor, *The One Minute Manager,*
Leadership by the Book, and *High Five!*

INTRODUCTION

W HEN JESUS CALLED OUT to the fishermen, "Follow me,
and I will make you fishers of men," he was about to
transform each of them from someone who worked only for himself and a daily catch to someone who was part of a larger team,
thinking about eternity. Anyone who has ever tried to get individuals to think beyond themselves knows that the real miracle
about to take place was as much in getting that sweaty group of
people to work alongside tax collectors and physicians as it was
in later breaking bread and feeding five thousand people on the
shore. The son of God knew that he could not do his work on
earth without a team, and you and I are no different. Whether we
are mothers, fathers, corporate vice-presidents, pastors, teachers,
health-care workers, or CEOs, not one of our good ideas will
become reality until other people embrace it and agree to help
move it forward.

Teamwork is truly what makes things happen, and leaders
today face their greatest challenges not in defining strategies or
getting updated information, but in getting diverse human beings
to pull together without pulling each other apart.

When my first book, *Jesus, CEO: Using Ancient Wisdom for
Visionary Leadership*, was published, it quickly became an international bestseller. I was blessed to be invited to meet and consult

with leaders from all industries and walks of life all over the world. CEOs of billion-dollar companies flew me in for private meetings, pastors asked me to kneel and pray with them as they attempted to increase their faith, bankers from Switzerland and car executives from Austria came to me asking how to incorporate Jesus' style of leadership into theirs.

I remember most particularly a letter from Doug Hawthorne, a CEO with fifteen thousand employees who wrote, "I am asking you to come help save the soul of our organization." I flew to meet with him, and am meeting with him still. Together we are journeying into the next phase of leadership, the one that goes beyond the coordinates outlined in *Jesus, CEO* and presents new insights into the pivot point of successful human enterprise: *teambuilding*.

All progress depends on this one skill, yet too few of us are trained in this dynamic. And for many of us, the old styles of leadership we *did* learn are no longer working.

I will never forget the tears in the eyes of one fifty-five-year-old CEO who looked at the dismal report card just issued by his 250 employees. As we sat in his New York conference room, he admitted that their low morale and performance had resulted from his autocratic leadership style. "I know that I am the problem, Laurie Beth," he said in a whisper, "but frankly I don't know any other way to lead."

This well-meaning, well-educated Christian man was coming up against what you and I are facing, the new dynamic that exists in organizations and groups today: one filled with high expectations, ever-changing demands, and an increasingly diverse workforce. While the model based on the patriarchal "My Way or the Highway" used to work when information was selectively maintained in the hands of the few, the Internet and technologies give anyone, anytime, access to a worldwide base of knowledge. This has leveled the playing field, and turned old models of doing things into dusty pyramids of the past, interesting to look at but incapable of motion.

Maybe you are a department manager who just can't seem to get your group moving in the same direction, or a health-care worker who is constantly being asked to get more out of her people in shorter time. Perhaps you are like a worker in a Fortune 500 firm who confided to me that the stress level is at an all-time high, as budgets are cut and expectations are raised for newer and better equipment, with fewer and fewer people to run and design them. Maybe you are like the mother of three children who recently wrote me, wondering how she can get her family to work together as she leaves the corporate world to take up her work station in her home . . . or the CEO who can't seem to get his top people out of their offices and out walking the halls, communicating face to face with their teams as he knows they must if they are to succeed.

Teach Your Team to Fish was written for you, because no matter how clever or spiritually gifted you are, nothing in this world happens without teamwork. Jesus knew that. He was constantly exhorting his people to "gather in my name," "go out two by two" and always think and pray "like One." Jesus' final prayer was "that they might be one, Father, even as you and I are one." In this prayer he was talking about union and communion, common values and purpose—all of which form the bedrock of an inspired team.

There is a Chinese proverb that reads, "Give a man a fish, and you feed him for a day. Teach a man to fish, and you feed him for a lifetime." Jesus came not to give us platitudes and promises, but to teach us how to fish—how to pull together like the fishermen hauling in their nets, and gather in a catch that will become legendary.

When your people are walking around in the doldrums, watching the clock and counting the hours, the insights you will gain in the first section of this book, "He Excited Them," will remind you that your calling is not just to lead, but to *excite*. You will learn through Jesus' methods how to

- turn work into cause, so your team will be passionate about what they do
- seek successful mergers and acquisitions among your team members, so they work together better
- elevate the dialogue of your team, so team members will communicate more effectively
- turn criticism into collaboration, for better results for both the team and your organization

Once you have your team excited, your task as an inspired teambuilder then becomes how to ground them, the theme of the second part of this book. Too many leaders think that pep talks and promises of benefits alone will prepare the group for great things. In this part you will be taught important grounding tools and techniques, such as

- teaching your team stewardship, not ownership, of their work, so that walls or work "silos" don't get in the way of working together effectively
- conducting regular internal "audits" to ensure that your team is working on the right track
- training at all levels of the organization so your team will feel truly engaged and further inspired by new learning and new achievements
- using cross-industry benchmarking to assess how well your team is performing

You will know you are an inspired teambuilder when the people that come into your care emerge as different people. As the slogan on "Mike's Hard Lemonade" reads: "We won't reveal our recipe, but ten lemons go into a room, and only three come out." How will your people be different as a result of their work with you? *Will* they be different? Teambuilders need to address these important questions. Which is why in the third part, "He Transformed Them," you will learn to

- turn pyramids into circles—which is a better metaphor for better teamwork
- go deep in order to go wide, so your team can solve problems better—and therefore have time to solve more problems
- be kind but not always nice
- forgo the gnat to save the camel—that is, make sure your team maintains its perspective on what work is *really* important.

Many teambuilders fail the final challenge, which is to *release* the team. Jesus gave full authority to his team to carry out works in his name, which ultimately became the real test of how well he had taught and inspired them. The fact that their work has lasted two thousand years attests to the truth of who he was, and how he taught them. In the fourth part, you will be challenged to do as he did, and

- turn everyone into recruiters—trusting the Larger Call to add laborers to the harvest
- keep things simple—always reminding your team of the business they are really in
- send team members out to do their work unencumbered—letting creativity and innovation flow
- hold everyone responsible for customer satisfaction—making service the ultimate priority

- release the genius of your team—freeing them to use their highest gifts, so you can use yours

Teach Your Team to Fish may take you into deeper waters than you have ever been in before, but then deep water is where the big fish really are.

"Follow me," Jesus called out, "and I will make you fishers of all people."*

Turn these pages, and let's look together at ways he built his inspired team, using tools that are being revealed to us, to use if we only dare.

---

*Bible passages not found in commonly used translations may be found in the *New Jerusalem Bible*.

HE EXCITED THEM

As I CAREFULLY MADE my way across the rocks that littered the shore of the Sea of Galilee, I marveled at being in the actual place where so many people's lives, and careers, were changed by the presence of a single man. I tried to imagine what must have coursed through Peter's mind when he looked up at the figure that was silhouetted on the shore, and heard the words "Drop your nets, and follow me." History records that Peter did just that. As did the woman at the well and the woman who was given her life back when the stone-carrying mob dropped their accusations against her and let her go free. Jesus had an incredible ability to excite people—causing them to take their lives and minds and hearts in totally new directions.

What was it that allowed Jesus to excite people so much? Was it pure charisma—the promise of adventure—the presence of God? Certainly it was all three of those, and more.

In this part we will explore some of the things Jesus did to excite his team. For example, he offered them a clear path to advancement, which in that culture was very limited, or even nonexistent. He turned work into cause, elevated the dialogue, and wisely used the power of presentation. He taught his team the importance of systems thinking, and how to run a "family" business. He turned criticism into collaboration and showed them the SQM Method: *Simplify, Quantify, and Multiply.* Most of all, he embodied the mission of which he spoke.

Jesus brought fire into these people's lives. Those who had once sat in great darkness suddenly saw a great light.

He excited them.

HE TURNED WORK

INTO CAUSE

I must work the works of him that sent me.

— JOHN 9:4

A S JESUS WAS WALKING by the Sea of Galilee, he saw two brothers, Simon who was called Peter, and Andrew his brother, casting a net into the sea, for they were fishermen. And he said to them, 'Follow me, and I will make you fishers of men.' Immediately they left their nets and followed him" (Matthew 4:17–20). And then he put his arms around them and began to show them the Big Picture, one day at a time.

Study after study now confirms that people function better in their specific tasks when they know the big picture of which they are a part. A recent survey presented in the book *Values Shift: The New Work Ethic and What It Means for Business,* by John B. Izzo, Ph.D., and Pam Withers (Fairwinds Press, 2001), reveals that 91 percent of staff workers at every level would like to know details of the budgets of their organizations, even though their paycheck may be only a very small part.

One of the main reasons people underperform in their jobs is that they don't know "why" they are doing them in the first place.

To understand why this knowledge is so important, consider an example from the human body. Science continues to reveal the higher intelligence at work in our bodies. For example, red blood cells do the same thing in the body forever, but they never tire of their work. The red blood cell's job is to take oxygen to other cells in the body and exchange it for carbon dioxide. In this nonstop activity the red blood cell is not depleted but in fact nourished by its "job."

Scientists now know that the red blood cell contains within it *the complete DNA code for the entire body.* In other words, it carries a map of the whole body in its structure even as it continues to carry out a single, specific, highly specialized task. Some scientists theorize that perhaps because the red blood cell "knows" the function of the whole, it can be content in its "micro" task, and perform it without exhaustion.

In fact, every cell in the body contains the DNA code or "map" of the whole. Could it be that God already knew what management theorists are just now discovering—that even the least part of the body performs best when it "knows" the map of the whole?

If you have ever had the privilege of encountering an enthusiastic janitor or a humming cook or a singing maid, you have probably met the equivalent of a red blood cell that does not tire of its task because it knows its energy exchange is vital to the organization as a whole.

The number three reason people now stay in their jobs, again according to John Izzo, is that the *mission* of the organization engages and excites them. People also leave their jobs because the mission of the organization *doesn't* excite or engage them.

Perhaps as we move into a society that is literally linked by the dynamic exchange of intelligence, we experience a greater need to know the "macro" plans of our organizations so we can be fully engaged in our "micro" tasks. This represents a huge shift from the isolated feudalism or smokestack industrialism that preceded us.

Leaders who believe that they can threaten red blood cells into doing their jobs are asking for trouble up ahead. The famous basketball coach Pat Riley says, "You don't have to yell at someone who wants the same thing that you do."

Teambuilders inspire people to look up. Jesus did this with Simon Peter and his brother Andrew, as well as with all his other disciples and followers. By revealing the Bigger Picture, he turned work into cause.

Questions

1. Does your team understand the "DNA code" of the entire organization?
2. Have you shared it with them, or do you think it's a secret between you and God?
3. Why would one part of an organization need to know how another part functions?

Prayer

Dear Lord,
Help me share with my "cell mates" all that I know of your master plan for us . . . so that they too can work with ease and nourishment and joy.

Amen

HE TAUGHT COMMUNITY

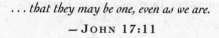

. . . that they may be one, even as we are.
— JOHN 17:11

JESUS SOUGHT TO BUILD community through expanded think-ing. His earnest desire, reflecting his Father's desire, was that no seat at the banquet table should be empty—that anyone who was hungry for the team benefits of right standing with God would be fed.

When Jesus gave a blessing to the Samaritan woman at the well, he was opening the door of commerce and exchange with a group that had been previously "off limits." After she had her ini-tial meeting with him, she ran back into the village and brought along her friends—multiplying the effect of Jesus' words. When he praised the faith of the Roman centurion who sought healing for his servant and required only that Jesus use his word to heal him, Jesus was opening up awareness that God's blessing and favor could exist outside the social construct of strict Judaism. He gave the example of a king throwing a banquet and inviting his family, only to have his family decline because they were too busy to come. So the king angrily opened up the party to anyone who was hungry. He did this because he wanted the table to be full of happy partygoers, rather than empty with self-righteous, self-involved people. When Jesus was giving his final prayer to God right before his death, recorded in John 17, he asked "that they may be one, even as we are."

Here he was seeking the ultimate merger of hearts and minds and souls — community.

Jesus had a huge heart and a big eye when it came to seeing the possibilities of unity among people of like hearts and minds. He wanted everyone to see their connection to each other, and to God. As I write this, there is a growing phenomenon called "coaching." Whereas coaching was once reserved for athletic teams, and "consultants" were hired to improve the profitability of companies, thousands of people are now working at helping others to achieve their highest and best. Some of the people I know who are doing this say that there is nothing as satisfying as seeing someone blossom into the truth of how loved and talented and bright they are. "When you are coaching," I asked one of them, "whom are you working for?" "Them," he replied with a smile. "And me. And God, too. And that is what is so great about it. It's like we're all in this one big company together."

Coaching helps people merge with others of like mind, and acquire new talents, often through expanding to the resources of the community. I recently had the pleasure of sitting next to Robert Willig, an internationally known economist who teaches at Princeton University. He was preparing a talk on Old Testament economics, and asked me what economic principle drove the New Testament. Not being an economics professor, I had to think about it for a moment, and then I replied, "Well, if you look at the early Christian movement as detailed in the Acts of the Apostles, the people sold everything they had and held it in common. They were instructed to use what goods they had to give gifts to others, and not to worry about what they were going to eat and drink." Finally I looked at Professor Willig and said, "New Testament economics was about mergers and acquisitions ending up in community."

Jesus built his team to think like a community. The benefits of such thinking were increased spiritual power, a sense of joy and praise, defense against impending dangers, mutual helpfulness, and deepened faith.

As I write this, I am in a cabin in the Adirondack Mountains. I've been invited to be the guests of Dave Cowan and Susanna Palomares, who are dues-paying members of the Fourth Lake community, which comprises families who own individual camps or cabins here, but come together to share facilities at the clubhouse on a weekly basis. Friday night is square dancing. Saturday night is charades. Monday night is children's night. Wednesday night is lecture night. And on the nights in between, someone will call and invite you to a potluck supper. In the afternoon everyone goes down to the lake, where they share canoes and kayaks and paddles and oars and life preservers and chairs. They take turns watching the children. It is an amazing thing. I have only been here three days, yet I know with certainty that if I lacked anything, I would only have to alert Jay or Albert or Loretta, and whatever I needed would somehow be provided. Arnie, whom I met at one of the potluck dinner gatherings, has come up from New York City, where he teaches a filmmaking class. He, too, marveled at the sense of community. "This is all we Jews ever wanted—to dwell with one another in peace," he sighed, taking a bite out of Katherine's chocolate cake. The Fourth Lake community has somehow successfully merged people of different ages and ethnicities, economic levels and beliefs, and brought them together around a very calm, beautiful, and tiny lake.

Gloria Gaither, a highly successful gospel singer and author, tells a beautiful story as she sits on the stage at the Praise Gathering. Every year, ten thousand people fill the Indianapolis Civic Center to bursting, as people from all over the country come together to feast on praise and worship, and listen to some of her husband Bill's corny jokes. When the spotlight goes on Gloria, and she gathers up her skirt and gets out the book, the whole auditorium hushes itself like a child about to be read a bedtime story.

Gloria tells about a person who was asked to bring a chicken salad to the neighborhood picnic. This person starts to grouse and complain, saying, "Sure — everyone else gets to bring ice, and I have to cook a whole chicken." Then the person eventually shows up, and finds to her surprise that there is an entire banquet laid out, almost as far as the eye can see — not only her chicken salad, but also fried chicken and cooked corn and mashed potatoes and watermelon and chocolate cake. Suddenly the woman realizes that "God didn't need my chicken salad. He just wanted me to come to the banquet so I could sample Bev's chocolate cake."

There is a lot to be said for one team's opening up to another team's talents, and joining them in a community banquet table. As Jesus said, "Happy are those who have been invited to the wedding feast of the Lamb," implying that we shall receive the benefits of two becoming one, the multiplied happiness that results from them doing so.

Questions

1. Have you had an air of exclusivity about your team?
2. What would happen if you were to open it up to others?

3. Why do you think Jesus' new policy of expanding the community threatened the religious leaders of his time?

4. What are some other entities that might be willing to share or merge their gifts and talents with yours?

Prayer

Dear Lord,
Help me get off my high horse and realize that the field is indeed ripe for harvest, and the laborers are few. Help me and my team develop an attitude of openness, generosity, and trust that will advance what we are doing, and bring about your glory.

Amen

HE GAVE A CLEAR PATH

TO ADVANCEMENT

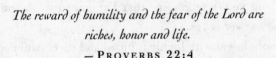

*The reward of humility and the fear of the Lord are
riches, honor and life.*
— **PROVERBS 22:4**

QUICKLY LIST FIVE CHARACTERISTICS that you think are key
to advancing in your company or team.

1.
2.
3.
4.
5.

This would be a good exercise to have all of your team members perform, as well, for it would provide instant feedback on
what they are each striving to display.

You might have written down, as I did, words such as *initiative,
assertiveness, knowledge, visionary thinking,* or *marketing skills.* When
looking at the career-advancing characteristics that Jesus laid out
for his team, I was surprised that the foremost was humility. That
word would probably not make even a list of skills that students

are being taught today. Yet in the Corporation that exists eternally, this quality is at the top of the list.

· For example, Jesus said, "You must become like a child in order to enter the kingdom of heaven." He also said, "The greatest among you must become the least." And again, "In order to lead others, you must become their servant."

Whoa! You might say. This can't be what it takes to advance. How can you advance when your head is down? Humility is . . . humiliating! I signed on for this so I could get the view from the top, and you're telling me that I've got to wash somebody's feet? The answer is yes.

The more I deal with highly fulfilled and successful people, the more I am struck by their humility. I will never forget the first time I met with "Jim," a multibillionaire who had flown in on his Learjet to meet with me. Having just sold his company for billions of dollars, he was most intent on discovering his divine purpose in the world. The goals of the business had driven him for so long that he was uncertain what to do now that the harness was off. Which direction should he go? Instead of seeking to make money, now he needed to distribute it. How should he best do that?

It was with some trepidation that I walked into the boardroom to meet with him. What did I have to say to a billionaire? Give him tips on networking? Tell him how to tweak his business card so that his clientele would like it better? "What, Lord, shall I say to this man?" I prayed as I made my way across the room to shake his hand. His red hair and warm smile immediately put me at ease. But what he pulled out of his briefcase surprised me.

"I did a little preparation for our meeting," he said, as he pulled from his brown leather case a blue spiral notebook that cost about $1.29, I figured. He had gotten one with ten divided sections. As we sat down and began our discussion, he opened the notebook to the first section. There, in ink, he had handwritten the words,

"I am the Lord your God. You shall have no other gods before me." In another section, at the top of the page, he had written "Remember to honor your father and your mother."

Tears sprang to my eyes as I realized the humility of the man sitting before me. He who had conquered worlds had come to review and renew himself in the ten basic Commandments — and seek God's will as if he were a little child on the first day of school.

No wonder he has done so well, I thought to myself as we began to talk. "The Lord's favor is upon those who are meek in heart." I have seen this form of humility many times since — in CEOs of entire health-care systems who still blush when anyone praises them, in brain surgeons who acknowledge that they are only instruments in God's hands, in opera singers who say that even birds have the ability to sing.

Paul Newman is one of my favorite actors, and a personal example of humility. He has given his name and celebrity reputation to Newman's Own, which, as you probably know, is a line of salad dressings and other food items, an organization which contributes its entire multimillion-dollar net profit to charities such as a kids' camp for the disadvantaged. In a recent interview, Paul, who is in his seventies, joked that he was going to stop making movies because his olive oil was now grossing a higher figure than his films. The quality that is so appealing about this man is his humility.

I don't know why humility would be a requirement for advancement on God's team. Perhaps it is because there is so much to learn that those who think they know it all cannot be trained. Perhaps it is because God didn't design the world as a pyramid of power, but as a revolving circle, dependent on the sun and moon and the elements for its seasons — with none taking precedence. Perhaps it is because a humble heart is a teachable heart. According to Webster's Dictionary, *humble* means meek or modest, deferentially respectful, low in rank or station. It comes from the Latin root *humus*, meaning "ground."

"Blessed are the meek," Jesus said, "for they shall inherit the earth." We are also told in scripture that humility

1. is the road to honor (I Kings 3:11–14)
2. leads to riches (Proverbs 22:4)
3. brings blessings (2 Chronicles 7:14–15)
4. guarantees exaltation (James 4:10)
5. ensures God's Presence (Isaiah 57:15)
6. makes one truly great (Matthew 18:4)
7. unlocks more grace (Proverbs 3:34, James 4:6)

Let's look at the examples provided in each of those verses. In 1 Kings 3, Solomon was told by God that he could have anything he asked for. Solomon, realizing he was facing a huge responsibility as king of a great nation, asked for the gift of wisdom, meaning that he acknowledged that he didn't have enough of his own. This humble request pleased God greatly. "Because you have asked for wisdom to rule justly, instead of long life for yourself or riches or the death of your enemies, I will do what you have asked. And I will also give you what you have not asked for: all your life you will have wealth and honor, more than that of any other king." Quite a payoff for being humble.

Proverbs 22:4 reads, "The reward of humility and the fear of the Lord are riches, honor, and life." In 2 Chronicles 7, verses 14–15, God tells Solomon that if the land is not prospering, the people need to repent of their evil ways and turn back to God (in humility), and then the blessings will flow again. "Humble yourselves before the Lord, and he will lift you up," exhorts James in Chapter 4:6. In Isaiah 57:15, God tells us where he prefers to dwell. "I am the high and holy God, who lives forever. I live in a high and holy place, but I also live with people who are humble and repentant, so I can restore their confidence and hope." "The greatest in the kingdom of heaven is the one who humbles himself and becomes like this child," Jesus told his team, in Matthew 18:4. "God has no use for conceited people, but shows favor to those who are humble," according to Proverbs 3:34. And finally, in James 4:6, "God resists the proud, but gives grace to the humble."

A friend of mine just returned from the funeral of a woman who lived in the Lower Valley of El Paso, Texas. They had taught a class in prayer together at their church, and my friend Irma marveled at what had happened when she went to her friend's house. "Angelina lived almost in poverty!" Irma marveled as she told me of the humbleness of her house. "I had no idea she was so poor," she continued, with tears welling in her eyes. "People in the church always went to her for help, and they were never turned away. She always provided a meal or a place to stay. I thought she was wealthy, the way she showed such easy generosity." At her funeral there were so many people that they had to set up chairs outside. The entire community where she lived shut down so that those who knew her could attend the mass. And the other amazing thing is that just as they were carrying her casket outside, a rainbow appeared over the little adobe hut that had been her home. Surely God was there to receive and honor her, and all who had been graced with her presence knew it. One of God's greatest was coming home, the one who had acted like the least.

It was the day before Passover. Jesus knew that the hour had come for him to leave this world and go to the Father. He had always loved those in the world that was his own, and he loved them to the very end. So he rose from the table, poured some water into a wash basin, and began to wash the disciples' feet. He then said, "I, your Lord and Teacher, have just washed your feet.

You, then, should wash one another's feet. Now that you know this truth, how happy you will be if you put it into practice" (John 13:1–17 [summarized]).

How would it be for a teambuilding exercise if once a week we all washed each other's feet? If this were done, how happy we would be, and how much more quickly we would all advance to glory.

Questions

1. What would be some modern-day equivalent of washing one another's feet?
2. Would your team be willing and able to do this? Why or why not?
3. If not, what does the future bode for your group?
4. Are you willing to set the first example, not in a shallow, staged way, but in deep sincerity?

Prayer

Dear Lord,
Teach me, show me, fill me with your humility. My only desire is to be near you, and I know you live with those who are humble. Be always in my presence, and always keep me in yours.

Amen

HE WENT SMALL IN ORDER
TO GO BIG

Ye shall find the babe wrapped in swaddling clothes,
lying in a manger.
— LUKE 2:12

THE FIRST COMPUTER REQUIRED an entire warehouse just to store it. And for all its size, only a handful of people could use it. It was slow, clunky, and not very functional. But, by golly, it was BIG!

Any of us who have witnessed the microprocessor revolution have seen computers and telephones get smaller and smaller. Yet as they have decreased in physical size, their power and accessibility have increased exponentially. In the economy of the twenty-first century, the race is on to get even smaller—with computers smaller than telephones, and cell phones smaller still.

The quantum physicist John Hagelin recently wowed a seminar I attended with his explanations of current theories of the workings of the universe. Apparently there is now a belief that the energy stored in the smallest particle of known space is more than all that expressed in the universe of billions of galaxies, each containing millions of suns.

In his presentation, Hagelin reminded us that our entire world could be destroyed by scientists releasing the energy in a single atom. As I thought about this statement, it struck me that much of the business world maintains a primitive approach to building power. The ongoing rush of mergers and acquisitions is like trying to get the biggest fire (the most energy) by piling on the largest number of trees (sources of fuel). Yet Jesus knew that in order to get big, he had to go small. He didn't amass the largest collection of people to try to change the world; instead he released the latent energy in the hearts of a few individuals, and the world was changed. Perhaps that's why observers saw tongues of fire appearing above the Apostles' heads on Pentecost. Each individual was set on fire from within, and through that process, Jesus' cause and mission was multiplied exponentially. He went small in order to go big.

The futurist Roger Cass has accurately predicted major economic events for the last thirty years, including the diminution of OPEC's power and the resurgence of a new economy, and the "correction" in the spring of 2000. The way this "seer" works is to think small in order to see big. Cass assembles data from multiple sources, ranging from passenger fares to trade prices. He treats each piece of data like a valuable fleck of color, puts them together in a mosaic fashion, and then steps back to see the big picture. Cass states that by working "granularly," you can get "a perception of things that would not otherwise be available." (in *Fast Company* magazine, July 2001.)

The chairman of Intel, Craig Barrett, said, "As a corporation gets bigger and bigger you need to do everything possible to make it seem smaller and smaller."

Which would you rather have — one Joan of Arc or ten thousand scattered soldiers? One Saint Paul, or two thousand committees? One John the Apostle, or six thousand pages of policies and procedures? One David, or a well-positioned army, full of Goliaths?

"And the word became flesh, and dwelt among us." This was God going small in order to get big.

Team leaders aren't scanning the horizon for the reinforcements to arrive. Team leaders look deep into the hearts of the people they serve, and set those hearts on fire.

Questions

1. Where have you been trying to get big by going bigger?
2. Where might the drawbacks or limitations be in that philosophy?
3. Quickly name six individuals who changed history.

Prayer

Dear Lord,
Help me see that all the power needed to change my world resides within you, and me, as a team. Help my team members realize the same thing for themselves, and for our cause.

Amen

He Elevated the Dialogue

But the tongue of the wise is health.

— PROVERBS 12:18

JESUS USED DIALOGUE TO elevate the framework of his disciples' minds, especially through his constant questioning and use of parables to illustrate life principles.

Consider the dialogues Jesus had with people he met. Take, for example, the woman at the well. "Hello, how are you, would you like a drink of water?" This is polite, civilized dialogue. The exchange could have ended there, yet almost instantly Jesus elevates it to a more personal level: "Why not go and get your husband?" When she admits she has no husband, he elevates the discourse again: "That is right. In fact you have had five husbands. And if you knew who you were talking to you would never be thirsty again." He quickly goes from a simple civilized conversation into a Big Picture philosophical one—elevating the subject from water in a well to the water that springs eternal from God's heart.

Because Jesus, a teambuilder, was willing to elevate an ordinary dialogue, this woman's life was changed. She ran and got her friends, making her no longer a shy, shame-filled woman but a bold recruiter. Some theorize that she may also have become one of Jesus' financial supporters, making her a philanthropist, as well. Her transformation took place during just a brief few minutes of elevated dialogue.

Jesus did the same thing with Nathanael. When he first met him he said, "Behold Nathanael, a man in whose heart there is no guile." This set the tone for a positive future relationship through a single sentence.

Have you ever walked into a room and had the people stop talking? If so, chances are they were either ashamed of what they were saying, or wanted to keep something secret from you. Your entrance into the circle shifted the dialogue. Does your entrance shift the dialogue up, or down?

At a recent business seminar I attended in Acapulco, Mexico, the corporate consultant William Isaacs did a presentation on the art and importance of dialogue. Briefly, he shared that twenty thousand years ago people believed in and practiced animism — often conversing with rocks and trees. As we moved forward from hunter-gatherer societies ("What did that stone say?") into agrarian ones, it became important to talk with one another ("Please move that stone"). Farms and fields needed to be protected, however, and soon our dialogue went from civilized to coercive ("Move that stone or I'll kill you"). Supposedly we have moved from civilized-coercive to reflective ("Where shall **we** put this stone?").

Isaacs was making the point that there are various levels of dialogue, and we move among them whenever we engage in conversation. Isaacs further pointed out that we often freeze people's identity by the dialogues we hold with them. As a group exercise, Isaacs asked us to think about who holds our identity through their dialogue with and about us. Parents, for example. Spouses. Bosses. They convey how they see us by how they speak to us. (Perhaps this is why it is so difficult for adult children to interact with their parents in new ways, or for adversarial couples to find new ways to relate peacefully, because they are frozen in low level, warring dialogues.

We are all too familiar with the rapidly descending forms of dialogue, such as this:

"Hi, hon! I'm home!" "Where were you?"

"I told you I'd be late tonight."

"You're always late these days. Are you having an affair?" Guess where that dialogue is heading — fast. *Down*.

Here's a parent-child exchange; consider the kind of relationship that is being formed: "Susan, I thought I told you to clean up your room" (accusatory).

"I did, Mom" (defensive).

"You call that clean? This place looks like a pigsty" (accusatory).

"It does not!" (defensive).

Here, the mother is using accusatory dialogue that casts her daughter in the role of a "less-than" defender, dialogue which can keep her frozen in that image for years to come.

Here's a boss/worker dialogue that does the same thing. See if you can rewrite it so that it goes from accusatory to engaging.

"Bill, did you get that report in like I asked you to?"

"No, boss — I'm still working on it."

"Bill, you may think your job's secure around here, but it isn't. When I say 'Jump,' you need to say 'How high?' Got that? That report better be on my desk in the morning, or else."

Do your rewrite here:

Dialogue either uplifts or depresses, engages or alienates, imprisons or liberates.

In a visionary leap toward teambuilding among nations, Mexico's president Fox also raised eyebrows, and caused people in three nations to go into deep breathing, by asking a single question: "Why not eliminate the borders between Mexico, the United States, and Canada?" Although even he admits the realization of this vision could be years away, he has elevated the dialogue to an entirely new level regarding *all* border issues, including immigration, human rights, trade, and drug traffic. Anyone working on issues in these areas now has a whole new perspective to consider.

Teambuilders train their teams to speak new words in new ways — to build new identities with one another through positive, reflective dialogues rather than fearful and coercive ones.

Quaker John Woolman was able to persuade all Quakers in the United States to free their slaves a hundred years before any other group did by having one-on-one dialogues with Quaker slave owners, one meeting at a time, for thirty years. He asked one simple question: "How can you justify this practice to your children?"

In the essay "The Servant as Leader," Robert Greenleaf wonders if perhaps the Civil War could have been averted if people had used elevated dialogue, rather than violence, to come to truth.

"Whatsoever things are true . . . whatsoever things are just . . . whatsoever things are of good report . . . think on these things" (Philippians 4:8).

Jesus elevated the dialogue.

Questions

1. What is the form of dialogue most often used in your group — polite, coercive, directive, reflective, accusatory, or defensive?

2. What four steps can you, as a leader, do to elevate the dialogue in your team?

3. What might the results be?

Prayer

Dear Lord,
Thank you for giving us the power of words. May I always use them as stepping-stones toward your heart and the heart of others.

Amen

HE KNEW THE POWER OF PRESENTATION

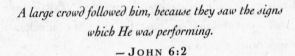

A large crowd followed him, because they saw the signs
which He was performing.

— JOHN 6:2

AT A STATE OF the World Forum meeting in San Francisco several years ago, I was seated next to the director of development for Warner Brothers. Intrigued by what he was doing at a conference devoted to spiritual values, I asked him why he was here. "Because I want to use the tools and talents I've been given to help make the world a better place."

"Me, too," I said, and shared with him a little bit about my work.

After listening to me for a few moments, he said, "I wish you would take a message back to the Christian leaders."

"What is it?" I asked him, making no guarantees of delivery (or receipt).

"They yell at us for not turning out movies that teach spirituality, and in many instances that's true. But they don't seem to hear us when we say, 'You cannot effectively teach people unless you entertain them. Putting white men in business suits and having them stand behind a pulpit and pound the Bible is not entertainment. You can't turn people on if they want to turn you off.'"

A rabbi sitting near us interjected, "Jesus certainly knew how to entertain people. He told stories. He had interactive dialogue.

He brought in props from the audience, like the bread and the fish. He threw things like tables when he got mad. He was an awesome entertainer as well as a great teacher."

A nun next to me added Jesus was *never* boring. But attend half the churches with his name on them, and you'll wish they'd put the kneeling pad not on the floor but on the top of the pew in front of you — to cushion your forehead when it hits the wood because you fell asleep. We all sat back and chuckled, realizing we were having this conversation in part because the speaker at the podium was boring us to tears.

God knows the power of presentation, and the early team members experienced it often. "In the middle of the night, Paul and Silas were praying and singing God's praises, while the other prisoners listened. Suddenly there was an earthquake that shook the prison to its foundations. All the doors flew open and the chains fell from all the prisoners . . ." (Acts 16:25–26). How about that for getting people's attention?

Ours is a very big God — with whales that leap and eagles that dive . . . yet we get handed little pledge forms asking for achievable, predictable performance. Who has gotten boring here? Not God, but us! Some of the churches with the fastest-rising attendance have given less time to the preacher and more time to the parishioner dramatists who are acting out modern-day parables, often with music in the background. Joan of Arc reinvigorated the fallen French armies by riding among them on a huge white horse, waving a large white flag, entreating them in the name of God to rise up and reclaim their country.

What about your team — what kind of rallying presentations are they getting? "Oooh — power point! Let's turn off the lights and go to sleep. We'll get the handouts anyway, in case the boss asks us questions later."

I was in one church meeting where the pastor took off his coat and tie and burst into a hip-hop song about the competition. The audience went wild.

Texas Health Resources, a health system in the Dallas/Fort Worth area comprising fifteen thousand employees, made a video short in which their CEO, Doug Hawthorne, did an impression of Jimmy Stewart in *It's a Wonderful Life*, acting out where the community would be if the company didn't exist. Texas Health Resources also takes cancer patients to a camp where part of the program consists of acting out skits relating to their hurts and healing, rather than listening to doctors drone on about new treatment protocols.

We are such multidimensional creatures. Why do we think we have to get one-dimensional to learn? "Okay, now, class, sit down and open your books to . . ." Jesus didn't teach that way.

Jesus knew the power of presentation.

Questions

1. When was the last time you gave your team an exciting presentation — one that was talked about even weeks later?
2. What would you need to add to or change in your approach to train your team in exciting ways?
3. Whom could you enlist to help you?

Prayer

Dear Lord,
From start to finish, you held their attention. Teach me those skills, and give me a heart that's passionate enough to use them.
Amen

HE TAUGHT THEM
TO BURN THEIR BRIDGES

Jesus said to him . . . "No one . . . looking back is fit
for the Kingdom of God."
— LUKE 9:62

CAN YOU TELL ME the name of the man who wanted to return home and put his affairs in order before he committed to following Jesus? Neither can I. No one saw a need to record it.

Can you tell me the name of the young man who slew his oxen and burned his plow on the spot in order to follow Elijah? It was Elisha, one of the greatest prophets in Israel's history. Because this young man destroyed the bridge to his former life as a farmer by burning his plow, he received a double anointing of Elijah's spirit, and went on to work incredible miracles in God's name.

Only people who are totally "sold out" to their ideas accomplish great things. Time and again I am reminded of a story that demonstrates the difference between belief and commitment: Many people believed that a certain man could push a wheelbarrow across Niagara Falls, but only one, his manager, was committed enough to get in the wheelbarrow.

The human heart has an inherent need for greatness — to be part of something larger than itself. But if we allow it to attach to lesser things, the heart will never reach its full capacity. People who pour themselves into their work are investing themselves in history, and they know it.

Article after article in *Inc.* and *Fast Company* magazines details the mindset of employees, especially those in the technology and the Internet industries, who are working long and brutal hours. Invariably they admit that they love being pioneers in their industry — creating programs and services and processes that will change history. One woman I know who works in a hospital has started wearing medical scrubs to work, even though she doesn't actually work in the operating room but in administration. She turned to me with a shrug and said, "Hey — it saves time. I've got more important things to do than worry about how I look."

No matter what industry your team is in, it must have something worthwhile to contribute, or it wouldn't exist. As a team leader it is your responsibility to identify that uniqueness and convey it to your team in such a way that lesser activities no longer have an appeal.

In the movie *Remember the Titans*, the character played by Denzel Washington takes over a formerly all-white football team (in the 1960s) and is forced not only to integrate it, but also take over the highly popular white head coach's position. As you can imagine, there is a lot of heat and tension, and the white and black players set up segregated eating and speaking policies, even though they are forced to play together on the field.

Finally the new coach forces the team to get up at 3:00 A.M. and do an exhausting run through the fields until dawn. They end up in the cemetery of Gettysburg, gasping and vomiting from the long run. The coach tells them, that "men died here from hatred, and this team now needs to learn to live in love so their deaths will not have been in vain." He also tells them, "I demand perfection. We cannot be perfect people, but we can be a perfect *team.*" And, indeed, the team ends the season with a perfect no-loss record. The coach had them burn their bridges to prejudice and mediocrity, so their excellence could take flight.

Jesus had them burn their bridges.

Questions

1. What affairs are you trying to put in order before you follow Christ?
2. How much of that is really a trap—keeping you from soaring?
3. What bridges does your team keep crawling back and forth on?
4. What bridges do you need to burn? What do they lead to and from? Draw and label them.
5. How would you act if you had nothing left to lose?

Prayer

Dear Lord,
You gave us no way out, but up.
Help us discount the value
of bridges in our lives —
bridges to the past,
bridges to judgment halls,
bridges to lists of our inabilities.
Make this team fully and wholly sold out
to You.

Amen

HE EMBODIED THE MISSION

I am the Light of the world.

— JOHN 8:12

TO *EMBODY* MEANS to give physical form to something invisible or incorporeal. Teambuilders must not rely only on their baton to conduct the orchestra. They must know each note of the music intimately and be able to hum it in their sleep; their bodies must "house" the music, and when they conduct, the music of the entire orchestra flows out of them through their facial and physical expressions.

You and I have seen authority expressed "in name only." In such cases, those who are issuing the orders have not earned the respect of the team, or do not truly understand the import of their words — yet they issue them anyway, simply because they have the title.

When Jesus said, "Tear down this temple, and in three days I will raise it up again," he was giving a clear message: "I am the mission. The mission is in every fiber of my Spirit and my being. Tear down the outer walls of my authority and the inner walls will spring up again."

Meanwhile the scribes and Pharisees were saying, "But it took Solomon thirty years to build this temple!" Their eyes were on the outward appearance — the tangible expression only. They were completely missing the picture and function of "embodiment" that was being presented to them. Thus, they thought that killing the body of Jesus would end the body of his work. History has proven otherwise—just as he predicted.

The very concept of martyrdom means that "mission" is indestructible—especially when its proponents have internalized and "become" it.

Osama bin Laden was foolishly mistaken when he thought he could destroy America by demolishing our tallest and most revered buildings. America's mission is embodied in the hearts of her people, and that can never be destroyed by acts of terror.

True teambuilders house the mission not only in their bodies, but also in their souls. If you took off the team jacket of Joe Torre, manager of the Yankees, would he still be a Yankee at heart? If you removed the company logo from your team's jackets, would the team survive? Would it have the same mission, the same spirit, the same drive? Or is the mission emblazoned on a plaque only, somewhere down the hall?

I have met people in priestly garb who emanated ambition rather than love. Some people seem to embody kindness, or confidence, or grace, while others may have the duty or title and yet emanate anything but the duties and office they are supposed to represent.

A friend of mine who works at a military installation bemoaned the new staff chaplain who came onto the scene changing schedules and structures on a whim, saying by way of explanation "Because I am the Colonel, that's why." If you have to shout your rank to get cooperation, you are not "an embodiment" but an "impediment."

I read that archaeologists in Italy discovered earthen vessels that still reeked of the garlic they contained hundreds of years before. The garlic had saturated itself into the very walls of the clay—seeping into every pore. Those vessels still embodied their mission hundreds of years later and were unusable for anything else other than what they were intended for. Could we say something similar about your bones one hundred years from now? Elijah's skeleton had so much power in it that when dead soldiers fell on it they leapt back up alive!

Recently I found myself sitting in a room with three hundred business leaders and consultants. It was a week-long conference, and the mild weather and resort atmosphere encouraged everyone to dress casually. At one of the keynote sessions, I ended up sitting next to a man wearing a green Hawaiian shirt, khaki shorts, and loafers without socks. He sat down close beside me in the crowded room as we began listening eagerly to the speaker. As the session continued, my neighbor crossed his legs, which brought his bare ankle within range of my pen. Suddenly I felt this overwhelming urge to reach down and draw a heart on his ankle. I repositioned myself to turn more toward the speaker, but the urge to draw a heart on this man's ankle persisted for the rest of the session.

Finally, when the session ended, I turned to him and said, "Do I know you from somewhere?" He smiled and said he didn't think we'd ever met. I said, "Well, I just have to tell you that during this entire session I was feeling compelled to draw a heart on your ankle." He threw back his head and laughed, then whipped out his business card, which had a big red heart emblazoned underneath his name. "My name is Jeffrey Smith," he said, "and my work involves helping people follow the path of their heart."

"Well, you certainly must be living your mission, because even my pen was responding to it!" I laughed, and then we each went on to our next sessions.

Are you magnetized for your mission? Could even children and animals pick up what you're about, even if you never said a word?

Your team certainly does, whether you realize it or not.

Leaders who embody their mission will not lack for followers. Jesus embodied his mission.

Questions

1. If you had to draw a symbol of your mission on your ankle, what would it be?

2. If your team members were to draw a symbol of the mission on your ankle, what would they draw? (Ask them.)

3. Name three people you know who embody their mission. How can you tell? Be specific.

4. If you don't embody your mission, how do you expect your team members to?

5. Is your current mission exciting enough to emblazon on every cell in your being? (If not, go find one that is.)

Prayer

Dear Lord,

Let your mission be so embodied in me that my very being shouts it out, without my even saying a word.

Amen

He Managed Remote Teams
Through Prayer

~~~~~~~

My kingdom is not of this world.
— John 18:36

Jesus offered his teammates the benefit of connectedness: I will move with you as you grow, and together we can suspend a rhinoceros in midair, if need be, or make a mountain move. And the vehicles that could make this happen were faith and prayer. Long before cellular phones were invented, Jesus was connecting his team in the field via "laser" communications. And the range was unlimited.

Recently I had a phone call from Bob Jewell, one of our Path facilitators in Ohio. He said, "Laurie, I've been praying for you every day."

I said, "I know you have been, Bob — I can feel it."

"Really?" he replied in awe. "Lately I thought my prayers were confined to a three-state area."

We both burst out laughing.

It made me wonder how far I think my prayer range is. I vowed then and there to renew my belief in the power of prayer to have unlimited range, and to be a bold and consistent transmitter, rather than a weak signal that broke up whenever a mountain appeared.

Technology has offered teams multiple ways to stay in contact with one another. Adobe Systems, a high-tech firm, webcasts its monthly "all hands" meetings. The sales force at Pepsi Bottling Group is kept in contact through a monthly video detailing selling strategies. The pharmaceuticals giant Merck not only sends out a daily printed newsletter to all employees, but has also launched a global portal site on its internal network to keep employees connected.

Nancy Duarte, of Duarte Design in Silicon Valley, showed me how they connect their multiple office sites and staff members. There are video conferencing rooms in all four locations, as well as Web cameras on the computers of team members. She also pointed to the life-size photographic cardboard cutouts of off-site staff members: "If, say, John in Chico is on a project with a team member working here in San Jose, John's cutout is placed by the team worker's desk, so they have a constant visual reminder that they are not alone."

"For the designer who works out of his home, we arranged dual day-long camera transmissions — so he can look up and see and hear the office ambience even though he's two thousand miles away, and can comment on what's happening as it's taking place. Likewise, we get blessed with a day-long mug shot of him at his computer, so we can ask him questions at will."

All of this connectedness is to help people feel — and remember — that they are not alone.

I will never forget Alma Trottman, who helped people register for my seminar in the Bahamas. In bold print, on her name tag was written ALMA TROTTMAN, REGISTRAR. And then, underneath that, in letters just as large, was written her other duty for the conference: INTERCESSOR. Before I spoke, I came and asked her to pray for me and the group again. She smilingly obliged.

When Jesus was apart from his team, on one of his final nights on earth, he prayed, "They were your gifts, and you gave them to me. . . . I . . . ask [that] you keep them from the evil one. . . . I ask that they be with me in Paradise."

John 17, from which the above quote is taken, is one of the most beautiful examples of how Jesus managed his team. He prayed for them — constantly — and he taught them to pray. How silly we are when we take out our cell phones to talk to one another, and yet are self-conscious and embarrassed about connecting to God verbally in front of others.

But not all prayer has to be expressed verbally and openly. Donna, a former team director for a multinational corporation, shared with me that she often volunteered at churches in foreign countries in her off-work time. One such church was trying to launch a revival, and had distributed multiple pieces of literature and invited several big-name preachers to help launch the event, but nothing seemed to be happening. Hearing of Donna's work with other churches, the pastor invited her to speak. She said, "I will not speak, but I will pray."

She gathered several of the church members, and on the Saturday before the event, she spent all day praying in the auditorium, going chair by chair. She said that at some chairs she couldn't just move on, but was called to spend several minutes of intense, concentrated time. After twelve hours, she and her prayer team left to rest up for the Sunday-morning service. When she arrived the next morning to a full auditorium, the pastor stood and said, "Donna said she wouldn't speak here, but I'm going to ask her to say a few words anyway."

Donna got up, took the microphone in her hand, and waved it over the crowd. People began instantly falling to their knees. Within minutes, the *entire* audience fell to their knees in tears and began beseeching the Lord to come into their hearts. As the astonished pastor looked on, Donna quietly left the stage. Donna looked at me and smiled. "Revival *did* come to that town, and I never did speak out loud."

Are you using the power of prayer for your team? And isn't prayer, after all, the ultimate communication technology? Jesus broke out in prayer constantly. He was bilingual that way—intermixing earthly language with that of the heavens, teaching his team to do the same.

He managed his teams with prayer.

Questions

1. What is your prayer range?
2. How often do you use it?
3. What and whom do you use it for?
4. Do you believe that prayer can help your team stay connected?
5. Do they?
6. How many languages do you speak on the job?

Prayer

Dear Lord,
Let your words be my words, and my words be yours. Let your prayer life be my example and my goal.

Amen

He Valued Results

Over Face Time

Blessed are those that have not seen,
and yet have believed.
— John 20:29

Scriptures clearly showed that Jesus would have been happier if the scribes and the Pharisees had spent a lot less time in the temple, collecting sacrifices and honoring each other with awards, and a lot more time in the field, delivering the results that compassion alone can bring.

"Why do you call me Lord [to my face] and yet do not do the things that I say?" he asked, voicing anger and frustration at those who should have been his top producers. They were giving him plenty of face time but not the results he wanted.

I recently spoke to a group about the importance of knowing your mission, and afterward I stayed to sign books. One man waited patiently in line for an hour, letting others step ahead of him to get their books autographed. When the others had cleared away, he sat down and said shyly, "Hi, Laurie Beth. My name is Paul." He paused for a moment, looking down at his book, and then raised his head suddenly and said, "I'm named after the apostle Paul, you know, the only one who never met Jesus face to face." I laughed in delight at his explanation, and then we spent some time together, refining his mission statement.

Paul's humorous explanation of his name was only partly a joke. This Paul felt that his work was really lacking in divine inspiration because he was named after someone who never actually met Christ — as if he were doomed by his name to forever remain an outsider, someone not good enough to be ushered into the inner circle.

What Paul the Apostle lacked in face time, however, he more than made up in results. Not even Peter, the one with the keys, could outstrip Paul in his zeal for spreading the Gospel. You might say Paul was the field representative who never got to shake the Boss's hand personally. But did that slow him down? Not one bit. Somehow his conversion experience, and the subsequent "e-mails" he received from Headquarters thereafter, were enough to assure him that he worked for someone who valued results over face time.

Jeremiah spoke of a truly nonhierarchical organization in the scripture when he wrote: "Within them I shall plant my law, writing it on their hearts. . . . There will be no further need for everyone to teach the other, saying 'Learn to know Yahweh.' No, they will all know me, from the least to the greatest" (Jeremiah 31:33–34).

These are the days when worshiping at Headquarters will be replaced by daily communion and an outpouring of the corporate philosophy, if you will. This is the hierarchy God longs for — the hierarchy of the heart. As a corporate director of Catholic Healthcare West shared, "When values are internalized, the need for rules diminishes." So also does the need to "show up" physically at Headquarters.

Today some 20 percent of corporate workers work out of their homes. Vice-presidents who were trained in the old school of time cards and a glass office towering over the workers on the floor are reluctantly being forced to allow (or even encourage) their top performers hardly to show up at all. In the next fifteen years, 70 percent of the workforce will be "nonpermanent," off-site employees, according to the Center for the 21st Century. A *Fortune* magazine poll of headhunters showed that employees most likely to turn down job offers at headquarters had flex-time (off-site) positions elsewhere.

Patricia Aburdeene, author of *The Digital Corporate Soul,* declared that the Internet is becoming so ubiquitous and unstoppable because it is a "mirror" of the way the universe works — unbounded exchanges of information, moving at faster and faster speeds — branching out in ever-expanding and unpredictable directions, with no "human" in charge.

The disciples whose mother requested that they be granted the right to sit on either side of Jesus in heaven, were not nearly as prolific or remembered for their work as Paul, a "field representative," who never actually got to meet the Boss.

Jesus valued results over face time.

Questions

1. Does your team have the corporate values written in their hearts?
2. Do you demand a lot of face time from your team?
3. Do *you* value face time over results?
4. Is your team clear about what those results might look like?

Prayer

Dear Lord,

Let me not seek to bask in the glow of my reflection in their eyes, but rather let them reflect you and everything you've taught us, through results that make you proud.

Amen

HE RAN A FAMILY BUSINESS

And going on from there, he saw another pair of
brothers, and he called them.

— MATTHEW 4:21

JESUS WAS SUCH AN incredible teambuilder because he considered the business a "family" business, and crafted team members into the family tree with a sense of fierce determination. He also treated the team as family.

"I always do what pleases my Father" also became "My father always does what I ask him to do." From there it became "Whatever you ask in my name I will do for you." Thus, team members got an immediate sense of having the same last name. This bestowed upon them not only an incredible sense of authority, but also a "familiarity" that people found hard to resist. People who worked with Jesus became part of his family.

The importance of treating team members as family is echoed in many of the reasons people join — or leave — a team. Either they feel as though they "belong," or they don't. Visionary teambuilders are at work — and getting results — in corporate America. An employee of Wegman's Food Markets in Rochester, New York, said to a customer standing in line, "I feel as though the people here are my second family."

Authors and researchers John Izzo and Pam Withers report that a growing crop of workers often have "unfinished business" when it comes to family and community. The authors write, "Many of them spent a great deal of time unsupervised and with much less focused one-on-one time with their parents than previous generations. Hence, the hunger for mentoring and recognition are much stronger. Younger workers, the X and Net Generations, are also marrying later, thus making friendship the focus of their community, and high on their 'want' lists at work."

The Book of Proverbs says that "wealth brings many friends" and also implies that it is wise to use wealth to make friends. One observer stated that the true wealth of an organization is not its web "server" but its family "web"—of social and emotional connections and interactions that bind people to one another and to the enterprise.

Almost anyone can assemble a group of people, hand out uniforms, and call them a "team." But for those who have tried it, the realization quickly surfaces that teambuilding is both an art and a science, and one way to accomplish it is to treat the team as family. Family implies ownership. Family denotes authority. Family means you'll be there when the others have come and gone.

Jesus was the first one in attendance at team members' weddings and funerals. He went home with them to dinner. He took them to his home. He shared his hopes and dreams and frustrations with them, in good times and bad. And he didn't dump or desert them when they made mistakes. "Who are my mother and brother and sister? Those who do the will of God."

Jesus ran a family business.

Questions

1. Do you treat your team as family?
2. Do you treat your family as a team?

3. List four things Jesus did that made his team members feel like family.
4. List four things you can do to make your team feel more the same.

Prayer

Dear Lord,
All I am and have is yours. Give me eyes to see, and a heart to embrace, the truth of my team as a "family," just as you did.
                                        Amen.

HE TURNED CRITICISM
INTO COLLABORATION

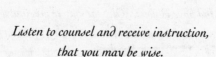

Listen to counsel and receive instruction,
that you may be wise.
— PROVERBS 19:20

MANY OF US ARE very quick to divide and categorize people, especially when we seem to have inherited, through no fault of our own, a group of critics on the team. Given the statistic that in large companies nearly *85 percent* of new employees are hired by the "human resources department" and not by the managers themselves, it is easy for leaders to secretly greet the new recruits with a groan. And as soon as one of them lobs a critique or a criticism, he or she is immediately labeled a "troublemaker" and cast aside.

Although this is a natural response, it is not necessarily the wisest one, for while some critics really do just want to tear down, others embody something vital.

Jesus turned criticism into collaboration on several occasions. When Thomas, his own team member, told the others that he doubted that Jesus had really risen from the dead, and in fact wouldn't believe it until he could stick his hands in the wounds, Jesus could easily have "fired" him for being a negative influence. Instead, Jesus graciously appeared to Thomas, showed him his wounds, met his need, and turned it into a lesson on collaboration and faith, saying, "Blessed are those who have not seen, and yet still believe."

Few people could have a more zealous or ardent critic than Saul, who actively sought to destroy the work of Christ at every opportunity. In Acts, we learn about the extent of Saul's criticism of Christ. "As for Saul, he made havoc of the church, entering every house, and dragging off men and women, committing them to prison" (Acts 8:3). Then Saul, "still breathing threats and murder," encountered the subject of his rage. "As he journeyed he came near Damascus, and suddenly a light shone around him from heaven. Then he fell to the ground, and heard a voice saying to him, 'Saul, Saul, why are you persecuting me?' And he said, 'Who are you, Lord?' Then the Lord said, 'I am Jesus.'

"Then Saul, trembling and astonished, said, 'Lord, what do you want me to do?' And then he arose — and obeyed" (Acts 9:3–7). When Saul heard the kindness and compassion in Christ's voice, something changed. His heart was smitten. And the love and vision and compassion of Christ turned Saul's criticism into collaboration — one of the most profound "turnarounds" in history.

Recently, Martin Rutte, coauthor of *Chicken Soup for the Soul at Work,* shared the story of two teenagers who were apprehended after desecrating a synagogue. In their vandalistic rage, the teens painted swastikas on the windows and doors, and turned over the tombstones in the cemetery. A very wise judge turned the sentencing of these two people over to the members of the congregation. Before taking any action, the elders did some research on the backgrounds of the youths. The fifteen-year-old male, a school dropout, had never known his parents, and had been raised in a series of foster homes. In an Internet search the boy had come upon a white supremacist hate group, which he joined, saying,

"They gave me a sense of family." The fifteen-year-old female, also a school dropout, was partially deaf and came from a broken home, in which both of her parents were alcoholics. When asked, she admitted that she didn't even know what the swastika symbol stood for.

The "sentence" imposed by the elders of the synagogue was this: one hundred hours of community service each, cleaning up and repairing the damage they had done. Both were required to finish their GEDs, and to write a full report on the impact of the Holocaust on the Jewish people. The girl was fitted for a hearing aid, and the boy had his two front missing teeth repaired. Both children were taken in by separate Jewish families to mentor and raise. At last report the boy was in the process of converting to Judaism, and the girl was starting college, seeking a degree in childhood education. Thus this synagogue of teambuilders turned criticism into collaboration.

According to authors John Izzo and Pam Withers, "When television's *60 Minutes* exposed the fact that children were using products by Minnesota adhesive manufacturer HB Fuller to get high," rather than deny or dispute the facts, "HB Fuller's team of leaders launched an extensive research and development effort to produce an adhesive without hallucinatory properties." In this way, they also turned criticism into creative collaboration.

At one conference with many notable speakers, I overheard a young man literally tearing them apart. His critiques of their style, content, and overall presentation were stinging and severe. Already nervous about having to follow this stellar list of speakers with a keynote address of my own, I promptly sat down with the young man and shared how nervous I was. I went through what I felt might be some weak spots in my speech, and asked him for some suggestions. I also asked him to give me a "choking" sign if I went off on a tangent. I further asked him to pray for me.

Guess who sat in the front row, beaming and nodding approvingly when I hit my newly polished rough spots. At the end of the talk he was the first to leap to his feet and lead the others to do the same. Afterward he said, "I am going to send you my entire database—free! I really believe in what you are doing."

I have no doubt that had I not taken him aside, listened to him, and given him some quality attention, I would have been just as savagely critiqued as the others. This was a critic who wanted to feel heard, and who proved more than willing to collaborate, if given the time and opportunity.

Obviously this won't work with everyone. Judas started out collaborating and then turned critic. It can go either way. But I would trade a Judas for a Paul any day.

Questions

1. Who are your critics on the team?
2. Do you know their backgrounds?
3. Do you know their heart needs?
4. Have you taken them aside and humbly asked what you could be doing differently or better?

Prayer

Dear Lord,
Please help me see all critics as potential collaborators.

Amen

HE TAUGHT THE SQM METHOD

Go forth, be fruitful, and multiply.
— GENESIS 1:22

AFTER MONTHS OF WRITING, reviewing, revising, and reject-
ing one business plan after another, I went on a search to
rebuild a team that had been decimated by the geographically
induced resignation of my number-two and -three team members.
(Since there were only three of us on the team, you can imagine
how this left me a little short-handed.) After interviewing a number of candidates for the key operational components, I finally
blurted out, "What we need to do here is simplify, quantify, and
multiply." There was a long pause as Marty, my consultant, and I
considered the clarity of the words I'd just spoken. Ultimately, any
team that desires to follow Jesus' teachings and approach to productivity needs to implement what I'm now calling the SQM
Method.

Simplify. Jesus took the six hundred laws of the Torah and
three thousand years of tradition and boiled it all down into one
Golden Rule: "Thou shalt love the Lord your God with all your
heart and soul and mind and strength, and your neighbor as yourself." Jesus simplified the rules. Previously, observant Jews had

tried to earn their way into God's favor by offering sacrifices, keeping the Sabbath, and obeying a host of rules, but Jesus simplified the process into one of faith and belief. He also gave them direct access to God the Father, bypassing the clogged switchboard of the scribes and Pharisees.

Quantify. By clearly defining the priorities of the Chairman of the Board, Jesus helped his team quantify their actions. If you want to know how you're doing on God's score card, just look at how you're treating the lowest among you. God doesn't want your sacrifices; he wants you to show mercy. If you want to count something, count the hairs on an old man's head. Pay attention to the details of those around you. Count the tears on a child's face, and wipe them away through your actions. God will not be counting your coins; he's going to be counting the calls you've made to the sick as his earthly ambassador. Jesus taught his team in detail what counts to God, and in so doing he taught them how and what to count.

Multiply. In the Book of Genesis, God told Adam and Eve to be fruitful and multiply. The multiplication talked about and emphasized in the Old Testament was biological. Hence we have books like the Book of Numbers to detail what a good job they were doing: "And so-and-so begat so-and-so, and thus-and-such begat whosit . . ."

Jesus shifted the paradigm about what kind of multiplication God had in mind. First of all, he said to go and preach to the Gentiles (not "the genitals," as one flustered lay reader pronounced the word in a reading I heard).

Jesus emphasized that the multiplication God was now interested in was that of spiritual renewal and re-creation, not who sired who. The fact that he remained single represented a cultural shift, as well, since all Jewish males were expected to marry and reproduce — even helping their sisters-in-law to do so if widowed prematurely.

When Jesus took five loaves and broke them and multiplied them, he was emphasizing the mystical and practical work the disciples were now called to. Multiply abundance. Multiply food. Pour out living water. Multiply laughter. Multiply joy by sharing among yourselves. "Go and tell others what you've seen and heard" was the great multiplying commission. Go tell. Freely multiply.

Team leaders of today must do the same. We must simplify, quantify, and multiply the work we are called to do.

Simplify — get to the essence of what you came here to do.

Quantify — determine ways in which progress will be measured.

Multiply — ensure that everyone on the team has the ability to multiply the good of the organization through every contact they make.

Jesus said, "Let your yes be yes and your no be no." He simplified. Jesus said, "Build up for yourselves treasure in heaven that will neither rust nor fade away." He quantified.

Jesus said, "Ask what you will in my name and it will be done unto you." He multiplied.

Jesus taught his team the SQM method.

Questions

1. Do you practice the SQM Method, or the "CED" (complicate, evade, and divide) method?
2. How and where could you simplify things for your team?
3. How, where, and what must you quantify for your team?
4. How can you ensure that each team member is multiplying, rather than dividing?

Prayer

Dear Lord,

In simplicity genius lies. Show me how and where to simplify, how and where to count what matters, and how and where to multiply, that my team may be a testament to your glory.

Amen

HE GROUNDED THEM

I F JESUS HAD PROMISED eternal life without preparing his
followers for death, he would have been a charlatan. He
would have been similar to the many get-rich-quick messen-
gers we see on infomercials, with their fancy cars and yachts
glittering in the background, saying, "We became multimil-
lionaires in three days, using these techniques."

Jesus didn't do that. From day one, he set his team's feet
squarely on the ground, even as he continually pointed them to
the sky. He told them up front and constantly that hardship
would be the price they would pay — that their social calendars
might dwindle — that even family members might turn them in.
He told them all this so that when the hardship came, they
would not fall away in discouragement and despair.

Jesus grounded his team in many ways. For example, he
taught them the principle of *stewardship, not ownership.* He taught
them to overcome cultural prejudices and begin to *accept diversity* in the kingdom. He *identified causes of failure,* and *practiced
restraint,* not unleashing his awesome power on every person
and situation he encountered, but only when and where it was
needed. *He conducted regular internal audits,* and taught his team
to do the same.

Jesus ultimately demonstrated how grounded he was when

he spoke these passion-filled words: "What shall I say — Father, save me from this hour?

"But it is for this very reason that I have come to this hour.

"Father, I glorify your name."

In the Garden of Gethsemane, Jesus showed that all his training was for the purpose of being able to stand up to this adversity — that because he had been grounded, he was able to rise to the occasion.

Teambuilders like Abraham Lincoln and Nelson Mandela and Martin Luther King and Mother Teresa demonstrated through their willingness to walk the hard road that their team members must be able to do the same. Teambuilders love their teams enough to anchor and prepare them for the very worst, so that when crisis comes, they will be able to say, like Jesus, "Shall we run from this hour? No, it is for this very hour that we came."

HE PREPARED THEM
FOR ADVERSITY

"They will whip you in the synagogues."
— MATTHEW 10:16

ONE OF THE GREATEST weaknesses in any recruiting effort is leading with a list of benefits. We have been conditioned to believe that the lure of gold is what will help us build the best and brightest teams. Yet history proves that people work for more than gold, and in fact will often work their hardest and best when they aren't getting paid at all — at least not in money.

Imagine what kind of response you would get if you ran an ad like this:

> Startup company seeking workers who will give up their personal lives, their families, and possibly their health. Work with us and you will get spat on, ridiculed, and maybe even killed. At times we will need you to work without any pay at all, and sleep wherever you can find a place to lay your head. We have no written policy manuals or instructions, and you will be required to find your own transportation. You may be asked to disappear on a moment's notice. You will work with IRS agents, former prostitutes, fishermen fresh off the boat, and a man identified as

an accessory to the murder of one of our first employees. Retirement benefits out of this world. To apply, contact man with beard prowling the seashore.

While Jesus excited his recruits with promises of perpetual prosperity, he also prepared them for adversity: "Listen, I am sending you out just like sheep to a pack of wolves. Watch out, for there will be men who will arrest you and take you to court, and they will whip you in the synagogues. Men will hand over their own brothers to be put to death, and children will turn against their parents and have them put to death. Everyone will hate you because of me."

He then went on to encourage them further: "If the head of the family is called Beelzebub [Satan], the members of the family will be called even worse names" (Matthew 10:16–25).

Jesus displayed incredible integrity in his recruiting efforts. Unlike many companies, which promise the sky and then deliver the dung heap to their employees, Jesus showed them the dung heap first, and told them they would have to slog through it in order to get to the sky.

One of the best-selling books of all time, M. Scott Peck's *The Road Less Traveled*, begins with a simple premise: "Life is hard." And then he proceeds to prove it throughout the rest of the book.

Apparently, God prefers to weed out the unbelievers before the battle starts. After Gideon was finally convinced that the Lord truly wanted him to lead the army against the Midianites, he assembled an army of some 32,000 soldiers. But then the Lord said, "The people who are with you are too many, lest Israel claim glory for itself, saying, 'our own hand has saved us.' Now, therefore, in the hearing of the people, say, 'Whoever is fearful and afraid, let him turn and depart at once from Mount Gilead.'" And Gideon stood and watched as 22,000 of the soldiers departed. Talk about downsizing! Gideon lost more than half of his workforce when the issue of fear was honestly addressed. Ultimately God weaned the army down to three hundred men — less than one percent of the total who were originally on the team. Yet they went on to victory.

John Parelli is a horse trainer renowned for his unusual methods of training horses to trust their riders, and vice versa. An ad in *Western Horseman* magazine shows him riding a horse with no saddle and bridle over jumps, around cattle, and in between moving cars. One dramatic photo shows one of his horses standing perfectly still as a helicopter hovers closely overhead. Another shows a man with an open umbrella charging at a young horse, one of Parelli's own. The horse stands there with his ears forward, unafraid. You can bet that the horses trained by Parelli are worth a lot of money, especially to riders who must expect the unexpected in their line of work.

One of my friend's stallions lost an important championship in Fort Worth, Texas, because someone in the audience wearing a red shirt moved. So, guess what color shirt the horse's trainer now wears. Guess who now moves around and shouts and flips open umbrellas and pops balloons, all in order to prepare that magnificent, intelligent animal for adversity.

The safety of our country depends in large part on a group of highly trained men and women who experience multiple hardships in various terrains during training so that they will not flinch in a critical moment in battle. Former Apple Computer guru and now "tech-evangelist" Guy Kawasaki says, "CEOs prove themselves in tough times, not easy ones."

John Chambers, CEO of Cisco Systems, states, "You should prepare people well ahead of time for disruptions in business cycles. We make this part of our culture, asking ourselves 'How do we adjust,' and use this as an opportunity to break away from (our competitors). All of us prefer fast growth, but you can actually gain more market share during the tough times."

I once read that people can handle just about anything except the unknown. So, by telling your team every difficulty they might encounter, you enable them to draw on their reserves of faith and courage when an unanticipated challenge arises. If they haven't been prepared, they may use all their energy dealing with the fright and confusion that the unexpected brings.

"I have told you all this so that you will not fall away" (John 16:1).

Jesus prepared them for adversity.

Questions

1. What adversity does your team face? Be honest about it.
2. Have you told your team up-front what to expect, or do you act irritated and surprised when they come to you for help during difficult times?
3. How do you prepare your team for adversity? Name three ways.
4. When is the best time to tell people about the hardships they will face? Why?

Prayer

Dear Lord,
Help me to prepare my team for the challenges ahead, so that they may be able to stand firm and unafraid, even when the devil's helicopter hovers overhead.

Amen

HE TAUGHT STEWARDSHIP,
NOT OWNERSHIP

God took the man and settled him in the Garden of
Eden to cultivate and take care of it.
— GENESIS 2:15

THE TELEVISION COMMERCIAL SHOWS a group of "suits" sitting
around a huge and expensive boardroom table. In struts a
young temp, who is holding a yellow legal tablet. She looks at the
group and says, "I want stock options, a corner office, a company
car, and my name on the door." The look on the chairman's face
reveals that he is going to have to give it to her, or risk losing "a
new hire."

Nowadays many companies offer stock options, or part ownership, to even the least of the employees in order to get a team
started. The escalating demands of skilled workers are causing
many a manager and CEO to lose sleep at night, wondering how
they can afford to chip off pieces of a company and still maintain
a profit and some modicum of control.

In an amazing news clip yesterday, I saw a group of nurses and
health-care workers on strike in California, demanding better
patient care, shorter shifts, more support. Their organizer said
that patients were in jeopardy because management, in order to

increase profits, is hiring fewer workers. The management came on the screen and said that the workers were jeopardizing patients because they wanted lifetime work guarantees. I do not know which side was in the right. I do know that premature babies were transferred to other facilities to guarantee their safety. I walked away wondering, "Who owns the hospital?" It seemed to me to be an issue of control. Yet perhaps the larger issue is not ownership but stewardship.

Recently I spoke at a leadership retreat for a hospital in the Adventist Health System. The new CEO was enthusiastically introducing me to members of his leadership team. He delighted in telling me little personal stories about his first encounter with each one of them, and I could see the genuine affection they all seemed to hold for this bright and eager young leader. When he came to a woman named Cheryl, he said, "I was amazed when I looked at her record. She has been at this hospital for twenty-five years! Go ahead and tell Laurie Beth what you told me," he said with a big grin on his face. She smiled and said, "I told him, 'Hello, David, my name is Cheryl. And I just want you to know that God gave me this hospital twenty-five years ago.'" We all laughed with delight at her assessment of ownership. Here was a director of nursing who was given the hospital by God, not by some legal document. And she took her charge seriously. In fact, in her mind, the word *owner* means *steward*.

Owner means "one who has or possesses." *Steward* means "one who manages another's property, finances, or affairs." There is a big difference.

Jesus tells several stories about servants who were put in charge of an owner's affairs. Given ten, two, and one talent each, the servants are told to multiply them, and are instructed to do so in the owner's absence (Matthew 25:14–30). In another parable he tells the story of a servant who owed money to the master, and was trying to figure out what to do with it until he returned (Matthew 16:1–30). In one of the first and most powerful stories about God's expectations of man, we are told, "Then the Lord God placed the man in the Garden of Eden to cultivate it and to guard it" (Genesis 2:15).

Here we see that wealth is placed in our trust so that it may multiply, flourish, and grow. It is not given to us for our own purposes. We are called to be stewards of the wealth, not owners of it. The clear understanding and application of this principle is what will determine how quickly your team advances.

Recently I was reading a magazine about legislative issues. One of the articles cited a movement by People for the Ethical Treatment of Animals to replace the term *owner* as it applied to horses with the word *guardian*. The reporter said, "We can only speculate how this word substitution will affect all of our sports and horseracing activities." What an understatement. "I am not the owner of this horse, I am its legal guardian. Therefore, before I can transfer guardianship to you, I must be fully satisfied that this horse will be properly cared for." Some of you reading this might scoff and say, "Ridiculous!" Others will smile and say, "Amen." Either way, the change in terminology would create an automatic change in attitude and behavior. Stewards or guardians act one way toward their responsibilities, and owners act in another. Stewards are accountable to a higher power, and owners are not.

What if every business owner substituted *steward* for *owner?* I wonder what kind of behavioral change that would bring? Bill Gates is not the owner of Microsoft, but the steward of its technology. AT&T is not the owner of telecommunications, but the steward of its technology.

When Jesus said, "To whom much is given, of him much is required," the concept he was clearly discussing was stewardship, not ownership. People who are hungering for ownership of the herd need to realize that they will be required to keep the night watch, as well as shear the sheep when the time comes.

I am working on discerning how this term applies to my business and me. For example, as an author I am not the owner of my books, but a steward of the information that has been given to me. As a consultant I have been given certain talents and abilities "in trust" that I will use for the greater good of God and others. Am I doing that? The answer to that question plays itself out on a daily basis. If I consider myself an owner of the material, as soon as the material is published, my work is done. But if I see myself as a steward of the material, my work continues until the day I no longer have breath, or the true Owner returns. There is a big difference.

Bill Pollard, CEO of ServiceMaster, a firm with multiple service franchises and 250,000 sales associates, continually tells his team, "We must be prepared for the One who comes asking questions." That is the concept of stewardship that is at work in this multibillion-dollar corporation. And the true Owner of the Corporation will assess the work of both management and workers.

If you can communicate clearly to your team that each of them is the steward of his or her particular department or talent, and that each will ultimately answer to a higher authority, then you will have a team of winners instead of whiners.

Jesus taught stewardship, not ownership.

Questions

1. Take out your business card, if you have one. Scratch through whatever title you were given and write the word "Steward" under your name.
2. Can you clearly define what you are steward of?

3. Can your team?
4. What performance criteria will the true Owner have regarding your handling of affairs? Write them down.
5. How are you doing with this?
6. How can you improve your performance in these areas?
7. How is your team doing?
8. How might they improve?
9. What will the improved performance look like?

Prayer

Dear Lord,

I am humbled by the many gifts you have given my team and me. Help us to be worthy stewards, so that on your return we will see you smile with joy and pride. We have much to learn about how to care for what you have given us, and especially for each other. Teach us again, every day. We pray in your name, the Greatest Steward of all.

Amen

HE USED CROSS-INDUSTRY

BENCHMARKING

The kingdom of heaven is like a mustard seed.
— MATTHEW 13:31

FOCUSED AS JESUS WAS in his intent to bring about a new way of relating to God, he was a master at using "cross-industry benchmarking." When he spoke about the kingdom of heaven, there were no references to halos, clouds, harps, or any other ethereal references related specifically to "the other realm" or the industry he came from. Instead he wove in stories from industries the people knew and understood.

When asked what the kingdom of God was like, he compared it to a mustard seed, or a huge banquet with an open invitation. He compared it to a good shepherd, or a father giving gifts to his children. He never related it to one thing, and one thing only.

The Pharisees, a sort of self-appointed quality-control committee, would try to "catch" Jesus in the act of breaking a policy rule. They would be looking at the fact that Jesus healed a man with a withered hand, and chastise him for working on the Sabbath. He would then turn and use the cross-industry example of a donkey falling into a ditch. "Wouldn't you help the donkey, even if it fell in a ditch on the Sabbath?" he asked. Not everyone there had a withered hand. Not everyone there had a working knowledge of the six-hundred-plus rules of the Torah. But everyone there had a donkey. So Jesus used an example to which everyone could relate.

His mind was like a magnet, drawing in examples and stories from every possible earthly source, in order to teach his team about his specific industry, the kingdom of God.

Teambuilders must understand that cross-industry fertilization is not only beneficial for their team, it is vital. Leaders of Daimler Chrysler in Germany are now experimenting with taking their leadership team on wilderness survival trips, to teach them cross-functional thinking. Other Fortune 500 companies are experimenting by taking their leaders to theater classes, sensing somehow that teaching them the elements of drama and performance will translate into increased productivity at the workplace. BankAmerica, Georgia-Pacific, and Lucent Technologies teach managers how to work better with their teams by having them attend music-conducting seminars taught by symphony conductor Roger Nierenberg. West Point cadets are taught leadership skills by being required to organize and run recess activities at inner-city schools.

A recent *Harvard Management Update* told the story of how a California-based company named Graniterock used cross-industry benchmarking to help improve its drivers' on-time delivery rate. The problem this construction and roadbuilding materials manufacturer was facing was that its drivers were on time only 68 percent of the time. Worse, its concrete was beginning to harden as the trucks arrived at building sites. A search of other similar manufacturers in the industry didn't prove helpful. Then somebody got the idea to reframe the question. The question was "critical on-time delivery." Who else, they thought, might have similar problems, although in different industries?

Dave Franceschi, manager of quality support for Graniterock, finally found a local Domino's Pizza manager who was willing to help with the project. How did Domino's get all its pizzas delivered piping hot and on time? Sharing stories provided the answer. Domino's Pizza relied on maps provided by the city's planning department, while Graniterock had long depended on another type of map that was known for comprehensiveness, but was proving to be outdated.

Second, Domino's plotted its delivery routes while the pizza was cooking. Graniterock now plots its delivery routes while the concrete is being poured into the trucks, rather than using the old method of having the driver climb into the truck and then get out the map. By studying the pizza industry, a concrete manufacturer took its on-time delivery rate from 68 percent to 95 percent within twenty-four months — considerably topping its original targeted improvement rate of only 5 percent.

Jesus used cross-industry benchmarking.

Questions

1. How narrow have you become in your team thinking? For example, are you using only your particular industry as a guideline for training?
2. What might be the benefits of some cross-industry benchmarking for your team?
3. What nonrelated industries might have overcome some of the challenges you are facing? Name five.
4. How could you attract or invite local leaders in those fields to dialogue with your team? What might you be able to offer them? (Lunch, for example?)

Prayer

Dear Lord,
Help me get out of my narrowcasting mode and look up and see the fields all around me. Help me understand the relatedness behind all things, and work to teach my team cross-industry thinking skills, as you did.

Amen

HE VALUED DIVERSITY

IN A WIDELY CIRCULATED e-mail, these startling statistics are given:

If we could shrink the earth's population to a village of precisely 100 people, with all the existing human ratios remaining the same, it would look something like the following. There would be

57 Asians
21 Europeans
14 from the western hemisphere, both north and south
8 Africans
52 would be female
48 would be male
70 would be nonwhite
30 would be white
70 would be non-Christian
30 would be Christian
89 would be heterosexual
11 would be homosexual
6 people would possess 59 percent of the entire world's
   wealth, and all 6 would be from the United States
80 would live in substandard housing
70 would be unable to read

50 would suffer from malnutrition

1 would be near death; 1 would be near birth

1 (yes, only 1) would have a college education

1 would own a computer

When one considers our world from such a compressed perspective, the need for acceptance, understanding, and education becomes glaringly apparent.

One has only to look at the colors of the rainbow or the myriad life-forms in the ocean to realize that God values diversity. Jesus certainly expressed this in his choice of staff — tax collector, fisherman, physician, former prosecuting attorney — to realize that he wanted a variety of personalities and backgrounds around him in order for his work to thrive. His welcoming of women into the inner circle was scandalous at the time, and yet he assigned to them the task of being the first to bear the message of his resurrection.

Despite all the talk about diversity in America, the fact remains that we still don't get it. One only has to look at the faces in government, in church leadership, and in corporate America to realize that the preferred color and gender is still white male.

A Bible story that has long intrigued me reveals that an early entrepreneur named Jacob figured out that encouraging diversity was his ticket to wealth. Deciding to separate from his old uncle, Laban, Jacob said, "Don't give me anything. But if you will do this one thing for me, I will go on tending your flocks and watching over them. Let me go through all your flocks today and let me remove from them every speckled or spotted sheep, every dark-colored lamb and every spotted or speckled goat. They will be my wages." Laban was a trickster who had connived an extra seven years of labor out of Jacob by hiding his oldest daughter under the wedding veil rather than Rebecca, the woman Jacob loved. Hence, Laban probably thought he was getting a good deal out of Jacob again, as he got to keep all the white goats, rams, and sheep.

However, Jacob devised a clever breeding program that caused the "minority" flock to multiply and flourish, causing Laban to inherit the weaker, inbred, all-white herds. Genesis 30:43 reports that "in this way Jacob grew exceedingly prosperous, and came to own large flocks, and maidservants, menservants, camels and donkeys." Jacob valued diversity.

American Demographics magazine reported that a study of diversity programs in the workplace showed that 78 percent of minorities felt that managers were not receiving adequate training in managing a diverse workforce. Fewer than 17 percent felt that managers were held accountable for the advancement of minority women. Nearly 73 percent of respondents said they strongly intended to leave their company due to the inadequate efforts of management to address their bias concerns.

In major metropolitan areas such as Chicago, Dallas, Orange County, Detroit, Miami, and parts of New York, non-Anglos are already in the majority. One-third of all scientists and engineers are Asian-born.

John Izzo and Pamela Withers report in their book *Values Shift* that Etec Systems, a manufacturer in Hayward, California, emphasizes cultural training as a customer skill. "Passport Day" immerses workers for ninety minutes in each of three cultures. Cultural training touches on geographic location; geopolitics; cultural values, roles, and relations; communication styles; and the effect of culture on business.

Fortune magazine states that "diverse groups make better decisions. If everyone in the room is the same you'll have fewer arguments and worse answers. Diversity is a distinct competitive advantage."

Implications for teambuilders are clear. Those who value the diversity of "speckled, spotted, and dark" herds will be able to flourish as Jacob did.

Jesus valued diversity.

Questions

1. How diverse is your team?
2. How prepared is your team to engage a diverse world?
3. What training have you personally received in diversity?

Prayer

Dear Lord,
All creation displays the respect you have for diversity. Help me and my team do the same.

Amen

HE CONDUCTED REGULAR INTERNAL AUDITS

Beware lest the light in you be darkness.
— LUKE 11:35

MAKING A MAJOR TECHNOLOGY purchase for a huge company has always been fraught with risk.

EMC, a software development company, takes its customer service operation very seriously. Rather than wait for customers to call in when problems arise, Nigel Anderson and his team of district managers begin every Thursday to prepare for "change control day" on Saturday. Each manager pores over every job scheduled to be installed the coming week and, with six engineers in the room, goes line by line over every step, asking the same question: "What *could* go wrong?" On about six out of every ten jobs, Anderson's team has been able to identify issues internally before they reached the customer. The result of this exhaustive internal audit? Customer satisfaction went from 75 percent in 1995 to 99.5 percent today.

Most of us have come to fear the word *audit*. It implies a bean-counting, jail-threatening IRS agent with rolled-up sleeves, combing through every detail of your personal life. The word *audit* means "a formal examination or verification of financial accounts."

Jesus continually emphasized the importance of each person and each team member, conducting regular internal audits to improve performance and maximize lifetime results.

For example, in Matthew 23:25 he accuses the scribes and the Pharisees of cleaning the outside of the cup meticulously while leaving the inside of the cup full of extortion and lies. "Woe unto you, scribes and Pharisees, hypocrites! for ye make clean the outside of the cup and the platter, but within they are full of extortion and excess."

He further accuses them of being a whited (or whitewashed) sepulchre (which traditionally engenders respect) that houses old bones and rotting corpses.

"Woe to you, scribes and Pharisees, hypocrites! for you are like whitewashed tombs which indeed appear beautiful outwardly, but inside are full of dead men's bones and all uncleanness" (23:27).

He again admonishes his listeners to conduct internal audits when he says, "When you go to bring your gift to the altar, if you have anything against your brother, go and make peace with him first, and then bring your gift to God" (Matthew 5:23–24).

In other words, you can't impress God with outward appearance and gifts when your heart is full of anger and resentment.

Nothing would reveal your misaligned state of affairs except a rigorous and honest internal audit.

Stories abound in the Old Testament about how an entire group of people could be punished because of the hidden sin of one person.

Jonah was thrown overboard when his shipmates ascertained that God was angry because of the disobedience of one of their members. "Then they said to him, What shall we do unto thee, that the sea may be calm for us? For the sea wrought, and was tempestuous. And he said unto them, Take me up, and cast me forth into the sea, for I know that for my sake this great tempest is upon you" (Jonah 1:11–12). Once they threw Jonah overboard, the seas became calm.

Because the early Jews believed so strongly that the presence of unseen sin could affect the entire community in a negative way, they developed the concept of the scapegoat.

The Day of Atonement involved a goat without blemish. The priest would lay his hands on it, not to bless it, but to transfer by proxy all the community's unknown sins. Then they would allow the goat to escape into the wilderness, and everyone breathed a collective sigh of relief as the animal carried their sins away (Leviticus 16:21–22). Attractive as this approach may have seemed, it did not do the job.

Each one of us is held accountable for his or her thoughts and actions, and Jesus was thus understandably adamant that we conduct internal audits in order to prepare for the coming of the true kingdom of God.

One of the reasons the Twelve Step programs are so effective in helping people overcome addictions is that one of the steps demands that people conduct a rigorous and honest inventory of how they might have harmed others in their past, and, whenever possible, to try to make amends. The founders of AA, the first Twelve Step program, must have known that in order to calm the outwardly stormy seas, the person must look *within*.

The comic-strip character Pogo said, "We have met the enemy, and he is us." I fully believe that 70 to 80 percent of our problems are due to internal, unacknowledged sin, if you will. Until we get aligned with God, we cannot move surely and swiftly to shore.

No team can succeed by always looking outside itself for others to target and blame. And no teambuilder can build a team unless the foundation is secure. Southwest Airlines regularly holds meetings at every level of the company to determine how well managers and workers feel the team is meeting the corporate values, and to identify steps to bring their actions more into alignment.

I wonder what it would look like if all our teams conducted rigorous internal audits. Surely, as we repented and stood clean before God, the peace and prosperity we seek would be waiting for us at the altar.

One of the world's largest technology companies, AES, issues a principles survey in which employees are asked to state how they are doing on their four goals of acting with integrity, being fair, having fun, and being socially responsible. The CEO personally reads every one of the twelve thousand responses. He is conducting a rigorous internal audit.

Jesus conducted internal audits.

Questions

1. When was the last time you conducted a rigorous internal audit?
2. When was the last time your team did?
3. Who is your team trying to turn into the "scapegoat"?
4. Why won't this work?

Prayer

Dear Lord,
You died once and for all. You washed my sins as white as snow. Help me to recognize that fact as I acknowledge them and repent of them, one by one. And help my team do the same.

Amen

HE SURVIVED

ORGANIZATIONAL LEAKS

And while he was still speaking, Judas, one of the
twelve, appeared and with him a large number
of men armed with swords and clubs.
— MATTHEW 26:47

JUST AS ONE OF a ship captain's greatest concerns is a leak
springing somewhere in his vessel, people who lead organizations often worry that the intense and often confidential work they
are doing will be revealed to the competition. This fear isn't
groundless, since leaks seem to be pervasive in organizations both
large and small.

People who are doing great work must realize that (a) leaks are
bound to occur and that (b) they will not prove fatal to your cause
unless you lose focus and stop or delay your work.

I love the story of Nehemiah in the Bible because it is so rele-
vant to teambuilders today. While Nehemiah was rebuilding the
walls of Jerusalem, there was a spy on his team who was regularly
reporting to the enemy.

"Afterward I came to the house of Shemaiah, who was a secret
informer, and he said, 'Let us meet together in the house of

God . . . for they are coming to kill you. . . . Then I perceived that God had not sent him at all, but that he pronounced this prophecy against me because Tobiah and Sanballat had hired him. For this reason he was hired, that I should be afraid and act that way and sin, so that they might have cause for an evil report, that they might reproach me" (Nehemiah 6:10–13).

Nehemiah perceived that there was a leak in his organization, and knew that if he reacted in fear and sinned, then his enemies would have cause to reproach him, and the work would stop.

We do not know exactly when Judas's heart left Jesus and went to the other side. Was it in the beginning of the work? In the middle? It certainly was manifested in the end, when he betrayed Jesus with a kiss.

Because of this "leak" in the organization, Jesus found himself bound and flogged in the house of the enemies of Israel, and at the behest of his competition. To all appearances, Judas won. But Jesus never took his eyes off the larger goal of providing abundant life for people through his own death. He never turned his face toward his enemies in anger, because to do so would have been to lose that focus.

When Nehemiah learned about the spying activities of one of his trusted construction crew, he did not halt construction of the wall and demand an investigation.

When a leak does occur, do not panic, do not fear, and *never* lose your focus.

Jesus survived leaks in the organization.

Questions

1. Have you had, or do you anticipate, wavering loyalties among your team?

2. What steps have you taken to guard against leaks?
3. Should they occur, how do you intend to deal with them?
4. What else might be causing you to lose your focus?

He Understood Mergers
and Acquisitions

And he told them many things in parables, saying,
"A sower went out to sow. . . ."
— MATTHEW 13:3

BUSINESS STUDIES REVEAL THAT more than 50 percent of all acquired companies fail to deliver the anticipated values to the acquiring company. According to the Houston-based business consulting firm of King Chapman and Broussard, Inc., these failures result from one or all of the following:

1. The cost of the acquisition was too high.
2. The acquisition was based on a faulty premise.
3. The integration process damaged the larger organization.
4. The process failed to achieve "integration of commitments" among the leaders in both or all of the organizations involved.

As I read this article, I was reminded of a parable that Jesus told:

"And as he sowed, some seeds fell along the path, and the birds came and devoured them. Other seeds fell on rocky ground, where they had not much soil, and immediately they sprang up, but when the sun rose they were scorched, and since they had no roots they withered away. Other seeds fell upon thorns, and the thorns grew up and choked them. Other seeds fell on good soil, and brought forth grain, some hundredfold, some sixty, some thirty" (Matthew 13:4–8).

As a team leader, you would be wise to understand that not all of your "acquisitions" are going to flourish.

The person who looked so good on paper, but cost you a fortune in recruiting fees, may produce results that are so temporary and shallow that they disappear into thin air, turning into birdseed if you will. ("And the birds came and devoured them.")

The person who showed so much promise early on, producing almost an instant crop of results, may wither and die at the first breath of adversity, leaving you with one crop and one crop only. ("When the sun rose they were scorched.")

The person who grew with you from the very beginning, laboring eagerly and willingly at your side, may soon become envious and judgmental, demanding more from you than you are willing to give. ("And the thorns grew up and choked them.")

All you can hope for is that somewhere among the team that makes up your field of dreams are members who will take root, flourish, and outperform all the others.

According to my reading of the story, none of the plants failed for lack of watering by the gardener. Teambuilders cannot take personally every team member's desertion or failure to perform.

I have spent many hours counseling CEOs, pastors, and entrepreneurs on this very subject. Just last week an entrepreneur met me with an anguished heart. Two of her key people had left in the dark of the night, taking several of her key clients with them. "How could I not have known this was coming? How could I have missed the signals?" she asked me, tears welling up in her eyes.

"Maybe it's not about you—maybe it's about the birds, thorns, and rocky soil of the human heart," I said, and then proceeded to share with her not only the parable of the sower, but also the story of Joseph.

Joseph's brothers were a jealous conglomerate who decided to do an acquisition in reverse, if you will, by arranging to have their brother sold into slavery. Joseph, the man who'd had dreams of sheaves of grain bowing down to him found himself having to bow down to practically everybody as he was led off in chains to a foreign land.

Israel's loss was Egypt's gain, however, and Joseph, through the continuous use of his God-given talents, soon rose to speak to the Pharaoh. He ultimately ended up overseeing all the resources of the country that acquired him.

When his half-starved brothers came seeking grain, they ended up bowing down to the very person they had betrayed. Here Joseph uttered the famous lines, "You meant it for evil, but God meant it for good."

Joseph could have spent a lot of time agonizing over how he could have been so wrong about his brothers, turning his back on them to gather water and finding himself shoved into a dark hole. But if he had, all that time and energy would have been wasted, because even though they meant it for evil, God meant it for good. Indeed, among all the seeds of Jacob, it was only one—Joseph—who grew up and produced a hundredfold. Yet this one seed produced enough to save and feed them all.

So, in your quest to build a team, remember why Jesus said some acquisitions would fail, and remember the story of Joseph, an acquisition in reverse, who was sold off, yet grew to be the most fruitful vine of all.

Jesus understood the nature of mergers and acquisitions.

Questions

1. Where have you planted your hopes?
2. Will you be surprised if not all of them blossom as planned?
3. When have you been affected by a merger/acquisition? What were the results?
4. How about a merger/acquisition in reverse, as in a divorce, layoff, or firing?
5. How might these examples strengthen your roots as a leader?

Prayer

Dear Lord,
You alone know the hearts of people. Help me continue to water all my seeds faithfully, knowing that among them at least one will grow and produce good fruit for all.

Amen

HE TAUGHT THERE WAS

NO "THEM"

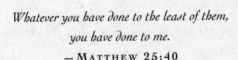

Whatever you have done to the least of them,
you have done to me.
— MATTHEW 25:40

ONE OF THE BIGGEST complaints I hear from managers is that they have a team of whiners and complainers. When this happens I do a visioning exercise with the group that at first makes managers quake in fear. I write two words on the board: "Less Of." And then I get a marker and ask the audience/department to call out everything they want "less of." I overheard one manager mutter, "We're going to be here all day." Surprisingly, though, the complaints in a "less of" form usually only last about fifteen minutes. I even stand there and ask, "Anything else?" and wait for a few seconds. At last it seems their cup of complaints is empty.

Then we go down the list and assign *I* for "internal," *E* for "external," and *B* for "both." Amazingly, it almost always turns out that 80 to 90 percent of the team's problems are internal ones that they alone cause, and they alone can solve.

Fewer than 15 percent of team blockages are caused by external factors — or "them." Yet quite often that 10 to 15 percent consumes 90 percent of the team's vital thought time.

I can't do this because of____(them.)

I/we would have been so much further along if it hadn't been for____(them).

Can you believe what____(they) are doing?

____(They) are threatening this entire operation.

How might your team fill in this sentence?

We can't do____(what) because of____(whom).

Now, imagine how they would complete the sentence if it were written this way:

Jesus, we can't do____because of____.

Satan, the most powerful force of evil on earth, was not what stood between the disciples and progress. It was always and only *their* lack of faith.

When they went out to heal the sick and raise the dead and cast out demons, but couldn't, Jesus didn't say, "It was because of Satan that you failed." (External.) He said, "Oh, ye of little faith. This kind cometh out only through prayer and fasting." (Internal.)

When Jesus went into his hometown and was thwarted in working miracles, the scripture didn't say, "He couldn't do much in Nazareth because Satan had a powerful stronghold there." (External.) Instead it says, "He could do no mighty works there because of *their* unbelief." (Internal.)

If you want to really get down to business, as a team, recognize there is only God and you. And then watch what happens.

Jesus taught there is no "them."

Questions

1. Name your "them."
2. Have your team name their "them."
3. Draw a picture of "them."
4. Now draw a picture of "them" standing before Jesus.
5. Draw a picture of "them" being swallowed up in the glory and power of Christ.
6. After drawing this picture ask yourself, and your team, What's keeping me/us back now?

Prayer

Dear Lord,
You are so much bigger than any challenge, problem, or imagined "them" I face. Help us to realize when it comes to powerful work, there's only you and us. Help us to see not "them" but "thee."

Amen

HE TOOK IT TO THE BONE

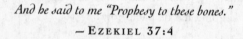

And he said to me "Prophesy to these bones."
— EZEKIEL 37:4

WHEN SIX MONTHS OF physical therapy, anti-inflammatories, and a cortisone shot still left my shoulder aching, I was advised by my masseuse to try acupuncture. As I lay on the table with a bright-faced, cheerleader-looking young woman inserting hair-width needles all over my body, I asked her to explain the concept behind what she was doing. She began talking about *ch'i*, which the Chinese believe is the energetic life-force that exists in all things, and permeates the world. She said my problem was due to the imbalance of ch'i in my body. "There are four layers of ch'i to the human body," she continued. "The outer layer of ch'i, which surrounds you, is like a 'halo,' you might say. The second layer goes through the skin and into the muscle, which is the layer we are working on with you. The third layer is in the internal organs themselves, and the fourth and deepest layer is in the bone."

"So these needles are increasing my circulation to the area?" I asked.

"Not exactly." She smiled.

"Stimulating the electrical impulses in the muscles?" I continued hopefully.

"Not exactly that, either. Ch'i isn't anything you can see or pin down."

"Well, you're doing a great job trying," I laughed.

I can report three things from my acupuncture experience. First, when the needles were in my arm, it became so heavy that I could not lift it. Second, twirling the needles to stimulate the ch'i was a mildly irritating feeling, causing my hands to twitch. And, third, when I got off the table I had 90 percent improvement in both relief from pain and increased motion. Whatever she did worked.

The corporate body . . . the team . . . possesses a certain "ch'i," wouldn't you agree? The outer layer is what the customer sees and experiences — the halo, or reputation. The second layer, of skin and muscle, comprises the daily activities and interactions. The third layer, or internal organs, are the operational forces in play, working behind the scenes to keep things functioning. And the fourth layer, the bone, is the mission, the knowing that supports all other layers.

The team that worked with Jesus, that stayed with Jesus, that accomplished what Jesus directed them to do, had a knowing "in their bones" of their mission and purpose.

Ken Blanchard and Sheldon Bowles give the example of a rock climber in their book *Big Bucks*. Looking at the mountain from a distance reveals only the challenge. Even getting closer does not present the exact "how." It is only when the commitment has been made to get up the mountain that the tiny toeholds and formerly invisible rock shelves present themselves. Once the desire to climb is "in the bones," the other parts of the body will help make it happen.

How did Jesus give his team an in-the-bones knowing? Through physical demonstration, through silent walks together, through taking them to secret and sacred places, by picking people with potential in the first place. I believe he recruited his team based on an in-the-bones sense of connection with them. People with no desire for a sense of adventure would not have followed Jesus down the street, much less to the cross. An in-the-bones knowing gives one the courage to venture into the unmapped places.

This past July marked my fourth appearance at the CEO International Conference put on by Debbie Bartlett and her team in the Bahamas. Debbie started this conference with one hundred dollars, a dream, and a team. Her goal was to expose top corporate leaders to the beauty of the Bahamas, and to expose workers in the Bahamas to the needs and work ethics of CEOs. Members of her church and people who had worked with her when she anchored the television news program volunteered to help her. They gave up their vacation time to help design programs, escort people to and from the airport, and wait by the tables to see if they needed orange juice or pen and paper, while the speakers from the podium poured their hearts out, exhorting the attendees to reach for the stars. The first conference was held in a nice hotel, which had a few problems. Some of the speakers didn't show up. Union workers held a strike. A promised support check did not come through.

Yet Debbie and her team did not give up. To my surprise, they held it again. And each time it got better — the speakers a little better known, the facilities a little nicer, the program a little more polished. This last year it was held at the Atlantis Paradise resort, which is one of the finest resorts in the world. Her speakers this year included the mayor from Atlanta, as well as representatives from international financier Sir Isaac Templeton. Her initiative to cross the Caribbean digital divide has been met with support from IBM, Microsoft, and the Discovery Channel. When I asked William, who has been my assigned personal assistant each year I've been here, why he gives up his vacation time every year to work so hard, he smiled and said, "Because when Debbie first brought up this idea at church, I had this feeling in my bones. 'This is right. This is good. This will work,' I told her. Somehow we all just knew."

There is a phrase in Spanish, *de hueso colorado*, that means it is so deep it cannot be separated out, it is "built into the bones." In-the-bones knowing is called faith.

Jesus took it deep with his team — exciting them, inspiring them, knowing them, and knowing *with* them, the good that was to be. Jesus took it to the bone.

Questions

1. If you sliced away the reputation, the assigned activities, the inner processes, and hit the bone of your organization, what would you find there?
2. Do you believe as a teambuilder that this bone is strong enough to support the future?
3. What are some ideas you have to get to the deep-down meaning and mission of your team?

Prayer

Dear Lord,
When they nailed you to the cross, piercing your flesh and bone,
you still poured out forgiveness, a desire for unity. Their bone-
piercing nails found only the triumphant cry "It is finished,"
as your breath ebbed away. Give me an in-the-bones knowing
of what I am to do, in you, and help me instill and excite and
awaken that in the bones of the team you've given to me.

Amen

HE TAUGHT UNUSUAL THINKING

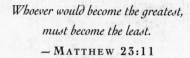

Whoever would become the greatest,
must become the least.
— MATTHEW 23:11

SETH GODIN, COLUMNIST FOR *Fast Company* magazine, states
that true leaders must ultimately realize that "you don't make
stuff. You make decisions."

Teambuilding and leadership is about understanding the key
issues and making decisions on how to act on them. Information,
after all, is a neutral tool. The wisdom to know how to use that
information is what is in most demand today. And wisdom
requires thinking.

Jesus was one of the greatest thinkers of all time. And much of
what Jesus taught was unusual thinking:

> *He who would become the greatest*
>   *must become the least.*
> *Whoever seeks to gain their life*
>   *must lose it in me.*
> *Unless a seed falls into the ground and dies*
>   *it cannot produce a harvest.*

The widow who put in a mite
  is richer in faith than all of you.
I must die
  so that you may live

In other words, whatever you think is "natural," isn't.

If someone seeks your coat
  give him your cloak also.
Blessed are the meek
  for they shall inherit the earth.
Blessed are they who mourn
  for they shall be comforted.

In fact, the entire life and ministry of Jesus was unusual.

In order to show that I am God
  I will become a little baby.
In order to show that I have the power
  of eternal life
I will let them kill me.

I am quite convinced that we live in an upside-down world, and Jesus was revealing, though his reflections, the way things really are. I see that unusual thinking is really the way to mastery.

Monty Roberts, a world-famous horse trainer, knows that the way to get a horse to follow you is not to chase him, but to turn your back on him and walk away. Mahatma Gandhi overthrew colonial imperialism not with armies, but with cotton threads and whispered words. Nelson Mandela helped set a nation free not by storming the barricades, but by allowing himself to go to jail and stay there for twenty-seven years. The person who led an army to overthrow one hundred years of foreign rule was not a wizened war hero, but a teenaged, illiterate girl. One of God's favorite games is surprise. I say it, and see it, all the time.

"My ways are higher than your ways," says God. "You cannot come to me through your natural mind, your vast experience, your supercalifragilisticexpealidocious vocabulary. The only way to approach me is by faith. And that is unusual."

Teambuilders must train their teams to learn to think fast on their feet, not to think in knee-jerk, always-been-done-like-that reactions.

> *When someone hates you, forgive.*
> *When someone persecutes you, rejoice.*
> *When someone____(you fill in the blanks here with your*
> *team's situation), then____(your ideal action).*

Leaders who teach and then trust people to think unusually—to think "outside the box"—will have a pool of talent to draw from when times get hard.

Sometimes teambuilders need to teach shy people to become more assertive—to move in the direction opposite their natural tendencies.

> *Jesus taught his team*
> *to reach out when they felt like hitting,*
> *to kneel when they felt like knocking something down.*
> *To pray when they felt like shouting,*
> *to give when it seemed there wasn't enough.*

Obedience is simply following unusual instructions. Unusual thinking, like this, is really the currency of the kingdom.

Designers for Herman Miller, world-famous manufacturers of office furniture, were encouraged to literally think out of the box (or cubicle) in designing the work environments for the future.

When their research revealed that in nature the 120-degree arc was the most common, they reoriented their designs away from hard ninety-degree angles into softer 120-degree curves, like a honeycomb, or even a hug. Their innovative rounded-pod designs, based not on "work" but on "nature," have won the company international acclaim. Jesus, also, thought outside of the box, even when he was laid dead into it.

Jesus taught unusual thinking.

Questions

1. List at least seven other statements Jesus made that showed his love for unusual thinking.
2. What kind of unusual thinking are you encouraging in your team?
3. When was the last time you forged new neurological pathways in your brain? In your behavior? In your team?

Prayer

Dear Lord,
Teach me to think as you do, even though sometimes it looks upside down. Help me create new currency in your kingdom, through bold new thought.

Amen

He Identified Causes

of Failure

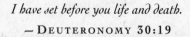

I have set before you life and death.
— Deuteronomy 30:19

USINESS ANALYSTS LOVE TO conduct autopsies on business
B failures. "What went wrong?" is a favorite next-day topic of
conversation. I would be willing to bet that 95 percent of business
failures today had at their root one of the causes of failure that
Jesus and scripture taught about, thousands of years ago.

Scriptures are designed to help prevent failure. They were
written in hopes that people would heed their wise advice, listen
and thus avoid heartbreak and failure. Those who listen to God's
words, and heed them, are promised prosperity and abundance, if
not in this life, then in the life to come.

So I thought it would be interesting to see what pre-autopsy
advice Jesus gave his team.

Certainly one of the key poisons for a leader and a team to
avoid was pride. Scripture lists several origins of pride, and seven
evils resulting from it. Let's look first at the origins.

It was pride that caused the king of Babylon to fall, as cited
here in Isaiah 14:12–15:

How did you fall from the heavens, Daystar, Son of Dawn? How did you come to be thrown to the ground, conqueror of nations? You who used to think to yourself: 'I shall scale the heavens; higher than the stars of God I shall set my throne. I shall sit on the Mount of Assembly far away to the north. I shall climb high above the clouds; I shall rival the Most High.' Now you have been flung down to Sheol, into the depths of the abyss!

Another source of pride is ambition, such as that displayed by King Nebuchadnezzar: "The supreme God made Nebuchadnezzar a great king and gave him dignity and majesty . . . but he became proud, stubborn, and cruel, he was removed from his royal throne and lost his place of honor" (Daniel 5:18–20).

In the book of Sirach, New Catholic Study Bible, St. Jerome edition, we are told that "pride has its beginning when a person abandons the Lord, his maker." In Mark 7:21–23, Jesus spoke about the dangers of having a heart given over to evil ideas. "For from the inside, from a person's heart, come the evil ideas which lead him to do immoral things, to rob, kill, commit adultery, be greedy, and do all sorts of evil things; deceit, indecency, jealousy, slander, pride, and folly—all of these things come from inside a person and make him unclean."

Self-deception is another source of pride, as Jeremiah warns Edom in Jeremiah 49:16. "Your pride has deceived you. No one fears you as much as you think they do. You live on the rocky cliffs, high on top of the mountain, but even though you live as high up as an eagle, the Lord will bring you down. The Lord has spoken."

Worldly power is also a cause of pride: "She and her daughters were proud because they had plenty to eat and lived in peace and quiet, but they did not take care of the poor and the underprivileged. They were proud and stubborn . . . and so I destroyed them" (Ezekiel 16:48–50).

Another source of pride is self-righteousness. Jesus railed against self-righteousness more than any other sin. In Luke 18:10–14 he tells the story of a Pharisee and a tax collector who went up to the temple to pray. "The Pharisee stood apart by himself and prayed, 'I thank you, God, that I am not greedy, dishonest, or an adulterer, like everybody else. I thank you that I am not like that tax collector over there. I fast two days a week, and I give you one-tenth of my income.' But the tax collector stood at a distance and would not even raise his face to heaven, but beat on his breast and said, 'God have pity on me, a sinner.'

"I tell you," said Jesus, "the tax collector, and not the Pharisee, was in the right with God when he went home. For everyone who makes himself great will be humbled, and everyone who humbles himself will be made great."

Now that it has been clearly established that God detests pride, let's look at some of the outcomes of pride. Among them are ruin, injustice, spiritual decay, destruction, hindrance from progress, and rejection of the presence of God.

Proverbs warns of ruin in chapter 16, verse 18, when it says "Pride leads to destruction, and arrogance to downfall." It again illuminates that pride leads to hindrance from progress when it says, "The most stupid fool is better off than someone who thinks he is wise when he is not."

Sirach, chapter 10, verses 6–9, states it beautifully: "Don't do anything out of injured pride. Arrogance and injustice are hated by both the Lord and man. Injustice, arrogance, and wealth cause nations to fall from power, and others then rise to take their places. We are only dust and ashes, what have we to be proud of?" King David observed that "a wicked man does not care about the Lord; in his pride he thinks that God doesn't matter."

What do all these warnings mean for your team? Could it be that at least some of the problems you are facing right now have their root cause not in economics or market timing or industry pressures, but in this one seed, pride?

A manager recently told me that he once had a key member quit because when it got right down to it, the team member said, "I either want all of the authority or none of it." Another CEO I consult with told me that when his company merged with another one, led by a woman, the top man threatened to quit his $350,000-a-year job, stating, "I have never worked for a woman, and I am not about to start now."

All of us are full of pride. But if we can identify it, admit it, confess it, and ask for forgiveness, the circle of progress and prosperity can begin to move again.

"He who confesses a sin, and asks for forgiveness, receives mercy. But he who denies it receives punishment," reads another Proverb.

We have all been affected and infected by the pride of others. Let's look at it, confess it, plead for mercy, and move on. Otherwise the tag on the toe of our dead team effort may simply read, CAUSE OF DEATH: PRIDE. "Too bad," mutters the coroner, as he pulls the sheet up over our head. "This team had so much potential." The entire team of the scribes and Pharisees was so full of pride that they couldn't recognize that anything good could come from Nazareth, and that God had chosen to deliver Israel by a simple carpenter.

Jesus warned against the poison of pride.

He identified causes of failure.

Questions

1. Name the three greatest challenges facing your team right now.

2. Ask the group if pride could be at work in any of these problems.
3. Where is pride hindering your effectiveness as a leader?
4. Have your team list all the origins and outcomes of pride.

Prayer

Dear Lord,
I don't want to die of poison — I want to thrive and pulse with life. Help us each become more aware of the pride in our hearts, and how it is blocking progress in you, to you, and through you.

Amen.

He Trained at All Levels
of the Organization

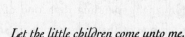

Let the little children come unto me.
— Matthew 19:14

"AND JESUS, KNOWING THAT he was God, and came from God, gathered together all the top leaders and CEOs from the surrounding areas and gave them a seminar twice a year."

I don't know about you, but I can't find a verse like that anywhere in my Bible. Instead, my Bible reveals that Jesus trained people at all levels within the organization (or "team"). He trained soldiers, prostitutes, CPAs, physicians, the disabled, priests, widows, beggars, and children. If you consider that the donkey he rode into Jerusalem was probably unbroken as it was a colt, the fact that he could navigate it down a long, winding road through thousands of screaming, palm-waving fans indicated that he even trained jackasses, too. Perhaps he had a bigger picture of "team" than we do.

In fact, it was the top layer of religious leaders that resisted everything Jesus had to teach. So, like the Living Water he was, he came up over, under, around and through them, reaching everyone who had "ears to hear," even the children. It is conceivable that Stephen, the first Christian martyr, killed under the assenting nod of Saul, soon to be Paul, was a child when he first heard Jesus speak.

Recently I sat with a colleague who, like me, conducts leadership retreats across the country. He and his wife were marveling that at a recent retreat the corporate leadership had spent $900,000 to bring in a very famous band for the evening's entertainment. "Laurie Beth," he said, leaning forward in a whisper, "I can scarcely fathom them spending that kind of money for one night! When I asked one of the vice-presidents about it, he said, 'Well, when you divide $900,000 by the total number of our employees, it only comes out costing about twenty dollars a person.'" However, all 45,000 employees were not at that leadership retreat. So who was the training and celebration really for? The leadership team members, of course.

Contrast that mentality with the training mindset of Susan Snelson, one of our licensed Path facilitators. Susan was brought into the Ukraine to help train leaders of the hospitality industry. After she finished her seminar with the top management, she asked if she could do a Path training for the maids. The manager said, "Sure," and Susan spent three hours of her own time helping thirty-six Ukrainian maids find their mission statement. "It was the most amazing thing!" she said. "What did they find as a result of your work with them?" I asked. She thought a moment, then said, "Their voice." She continued, "No one had ever paid that kind of attention to them before. And after they each repeated their mission statement, you know what they added?" "What?" I asked. "'And I work for the Ukrainian Hotel!'" Susan replied.

"Susan," I said with a smile, "Jesus would look at you and say, 'Well done, thou good and faithful servant.'" Susan wanted to train at all levels of the organization.

Cardone Industries, a huge car-parts and battery remanufacturing plant in Philadelphia, runs ongoing classes in literacy, money management, and foreign languages for its five thousand multinational workers. ServiceMaster does the same, helping train its 250,000 associates in basic life-management skills, as well as work required for the job. The American Bible Society allocates fifteen hundred training dollars per employee per year—*all* employees. SAS Institute, the nation's largest independently owned software corporation, has incorporated on-site child care and preschool training for the seven hundred children of its five thousand employees. Turnover rate at SAS is among the lowest in the industry.

Dyson Appliances Limited, a vacuum cleaner company and the fastest-growing manufacturer in Great Britain, has an unusual policy: on the first day of their employment, all new hires—no matter what their title—are taught to build a vacuum cleaner from start to finish. In so doing the leadership is communicating to the team that all workers are geniuses, that everyone is expected to have inside-out product knowledge, and that anyone can be called upon to do the job when needed in order to serve the customer. Dyson also has assembly-line workers switch places on the line every forty-five minutes, so they won't get bored.

Studies reveal that a child's mind operates at virtually every level of consciousness. Tests that can detect brain activity in various regions of the brain indicate nearly 100-percent usage of brain cells in the infant stages. As we grow from infancy to adulthood, however, these tests show that we use fewer and fewer brain cells.

Organizationally speaking, it could be said that entry-level workers are the "infants" on a team, while leaders at the top are the "adults." It might make sense to invest more training dollars at the head, to ensure that the leaders' minds remain open and fully engaged.

But training is not an either/or situation. Jesus said, "Unless you become like a child, you cannot enter the kingdom of God." In other words, massive retraining will be required, and all of your brain cells — at every level — must be activated and rewired.

I have spoken with many CEOs who lament that there is no "boot camp" for them when they reach the top. They are already expected to know, when really they want to continue to learn. Just like little children.

Jesus trained at all levels of the organization.

Questions

1. What kind of training are you providing, and to whom?
2. Look at an organizational chart of your team. Allocate hours of training given per each layer. Is it proportionate?
3. Name three kinds of training Jesus conducted in his organization.
4. Compare his training methods with yours.
5. Where could you improve?

Prayer

Dear Lord,
You taught children, servants, soldiers, prostitutes, and tax collectors. Help me do the same.

Amen

HE PRACTICED RESTRAINT

And to your knowledge, add self-control.
— 2 PETER 1:6

NOT TOO LONG AGO a well-known basketball coach was fired after publicly attempting to strangle one of his team players. There is not one teambuilder among us who has not at times felt a similar impulse. Self-restraint is as important as passion in getting a team to grow.

I have often wondered at the times Jesus said, "I have more to tell you." Until recently I always felt that those words were a measure of his ever-unfolding, awesome knowledge. Yet now I have come to view them equally as a measure of his self-restraint.

Imagine what it must have felt like to stand in front of a broken human being, knowing that you held the power to make him instantly whole — and yet choosing to ask his permission first, testing his readiness to receive what you knew he needed?

As someone who has been accused of watering a garden with a fire hose, this learning of self-restraint has been (and remains) a challenge for me. "Look — I have water. Plants need water. I turned on the water and watered them. What's the problem?" I have asked my angel(s) more than once as we stood surveying entire swaths of flood damage — areas flooded by me and my well-intentioned but not properly restrained ways.

"Discipline has purple reins" reads an ancient proverb. Since purple is the color of royalty, the implication is that embracing discipline will lead a person to the throne.

A writer once shared with me that good drama depends as much on what is *not* said and done as on what is actually played out. It is the tension that sustains drama, not the acting out. The essential principle that all physicians are taught is, "First, do no harm." Armed with an arsenal of potions, scalpels, prescription pads, and referring sources, a good doctor must approach each case, each patient, with incredible self-restraint.

When Jesus told his disciples not to worry about what they were going to say, he was cautioning them against boning up on illusory phrases or impressive words or memorized speeches in order to accomplish the work of the Kingdom. "Practice the self-restraint of listening," he was saying. "Engage the wisdom of the Holy Spirit before you open your mouth," he was teaching. To be a good teambuilder, you must first be master of your own energies and impulses and knee-jerk reactions. This is hard. One of my new restraining filters is the question, Is this a thought or an impulse? Wisdom knows the difference.

I will never forget the joy I felt one day as a friend and I were riding horses with my two Animal Rescue dogs, Chula, a yellow Labrador, and Joshua, a Labrador-Dalmatian mix. As we were moving along through the fields, a cat suddenly jumped up out of the cotton and began dashing off. Both dogs sprang instantly into chase mode, and began tearing off after the terrified feline. I stood up in my stirrups and yelled, "Stop!" Instantly (and to my amazement) both dogs froze and waited for me to come riding up to them. Trembling as they were at having been interrupted from their chase, they nevertheless displayed a desire to please me that outweighed their natural instincts. "Wow!" said the person who was riding with me. "How did you get them to do that?" "Three years of loving them," I replied. It was the only answer I knew.

Any animal trainer will tell you that one of the first and most important lessons is "stop." My father told me when he was teaching me to drive, "The *first* thing you should do when you get into a new car is test the brakes," he said. "It's the brakes, not the gas pedal that will save your life."

Teambuilders must learn to apply their own brakes. Words released in anger and frustration can wound the spirit of a coworker. One successful CEO I know writes out angry memos, and then filters them through her secretary before sending them — allowing both venting and braking to occur.

During the Gulf War, Israel demonstrated incredible self-restraint, deliberately not responding in kind to Iraqi missiles. By putting the brakes on its team's capacity for retaliation, a quick resolution was brought about.

In their book *From Chaos to Coherence: The Power to Change Performance,* authors Doc Childre and Bruce Cryer write that organizations must realize that "the unbridled acquisition of knowledge is a pale substitute for the seasoned maturity of wisdom." They acknowledge that we are overloaded with information, and that wise leaders help their team members understand the importance of emotional management, as well as information management, in order to succeed. Childre and Cryer also write that in the human body the parasympathetic nervous system is the one that slows or relaxes bodily function, similar to the brakes in a car. Researchers now know that multiple disorders and diseases stem from the diminished capacity of this system. In other words, the body's inability to demonstrate restraint of stress leads to disease.

In an organization, the team leader must exemplify this function, or burnout at all levels might occur.

Jesus did the same when he urged Peter to put up his sword. He demonstrated to his team members that reactive behavior is not the mark of a grounded teambuilder. "And before his accusers he answered not a word."

Jesus practiced restraint.

Questions

1. As a teambuilder and coach, where and how do you use restraint?
2. When in the past have you not done so, and regretted it?
3. Why is the self-restraint of the coach critical to a team's growth?

Prayer

Dear Lord,
Help me cultivate the discipline and restraint of cultivation, rather than fall prey to the ease of clear-cutting the forest just because I can do it.

Amen

HE TRANSFORMED THEM

I ONCE TOOK A cocoon on a broken-off twig and kept it in an open jar in my room, watching and waiting patiently until the day I came home from school and found a butterfly.

My friend Susanna Palomares took an avocado pit and grew it in water on her windowsill. One day I came to visit her and sat underneath its shade—two years after it outgrew its jar.

The miracle of transformation is everywhere around us. From eggs to chicks, from seeds to forests, from sketch to masterpiece, the whole universe sings that transformation is God's will.

The truth is we are all changing into something. The question is, into what? And for whom?

I recently watched a thirty-year-old, self-described "doomed to be an old maid" friend of mine fall in love at a Christmas party, marry, and two years later walk into my house a femme fatale—glowing and radiant and adored—transformed from someone who felt unwanted into the queen of a newly discovered castle. She was transformed by the love of her husband, who reflected back to her God's love.

Leaders can transform companies, schools, governments, and nations, through their policies and words. Teambuilders do the same.

But the transformation does not take place by adding new clothes to paper dolls. Transformation is truly an inside job. Jesus gave us his formula for turning cocoons into butterflies, avocado pits into shade trees, downcast women into glowing brides. It is a formula we teambuilders must take to heart: "If you make my words your home, you will indeed be my disciples, and you will come to know the truth, and the truth will set you free" (John 8:31–32).

He Taught Transformation,
Not Transactions

Follow me, and I will make you fishers of men.
— Matthew 4:19

TRANSACTIONS ARE LATERAL EXCHANGES between people — be it goods or services. Transactions occur every time two people engage in commerce of any kind. I give you this in exchange for that. Transactions are obvious and literal, commonplace and easy to spot. In contrast, transformations are invisible, uplifting, transcendent experiences that involve a fundamental shift or change.

Most transactions occur because people are seeking transformation. The drug deal that takes place in a backlit alley is a transaction, an exchange of goods, for a desired transformation. The person buying the drugs is seeking transformation from one state of mind to another. The cosmetics industry is a multibillion-dollar enterprise that has women lining up at counters, transacting for mascara or makeup, because they are seeking transformation from feeling plain to feeling beautiful.

Successful teams are those that understand that the desired end product is transformation, not transactions. Jesus embodied this principle in every encounter.

In an earlier chapter, I mentioned Jesus elevating the dialogue when he met the woman at the well. She had come to the well for a simple transaction — getting water in her bucket. But notice how Jesus turned this simple exchange into a *transformational* experience for her.

"A woman of Samaria came to draw water. Jesus, being weary from his journey, said to her, 'Give me a drink.' For his disciples had gone away into the city to buy food. Then the woman of Samaria said to him, 'How is that you, being a Jew, ask a drink from me, a Samaritan woman?' For Jews have no dealings with Samaritans. Jesus answered and said to her, 'If you knew the gift of God, and who it is who says to you, Give me a drink, you would have asked him, and he would have given you living water.'" Jesus went on to explain, "Whoever drinks of this water will thirst again, but whoever drinks of the water that I shall give will never thirst. But the water that I shall give him will become a fountain of water springing up into everlasting life." The woman then said to him, "Give me this water, that I may not thirst again." After a few more rounds of discussion, the woman "went into the city, and said to the men, 'Come, see a man who told me all the things that I ever did. Could this be the Christ?' Then they went out of the city and came to him" (John 4:7–15, 28).

Clearly this woman who came to the well seeking a simple transaction encountered transformation instead. In this quiet exchange, which could have lasted only a few minutes, the woman received several transformations:

1. a new self-image, from an undesirable Samaritan to the equal of a Jew;
2. from a lowly woman not to be addressed, to an equal associate worthy of lengthy attention;

3. from an outcast stranger to a newly forgiven team member whose heart was truly known;

4. from someone who was bound to dust to someone who was bound for glory.

A shy woman, head down, seeking water, was transformed into an emboldened champion and evangelist, urging everyone she knew to look up and see the real Transformation that was about to occur.

Jesus' team witnessed the effect of this transformation. It was one of many they were to see. In fact, Jesus recruited the first of his team members by promising them transformations, not transactions. "Follow me, and I will make you fishers of men." You will go from hauling in fish to hauling in souls, was the promise, and it was such a powerful one that they gave up the only work they had ever known to begin work they'd never imagined.

In a form of reverse transformation, Jesus took a group of more than five thousand people who had come hungering only for the word of God, and gave them food to nourish their physical bodies as well. The man with the withered hand received not only a new, fully functioning model, but forgiveness of sins as well.

Nobody got only a one-shot transaction with Jesus — not even the people who killed him. Simple transaction: take a body and kill it. Receive instead, a Body that resurrects itself and prays for your forgiveness in the process.

I sat recently with one of the vice-presidents of a multimillion-dollar resort hotel. We were discussing the challenges facing this entity, which had come to a foreign country and hired five thousand people on the island before they even opened the doors. Despite spending nearly a billion dollars to develop this resort, the owners were now facing multiple complaints from hostile and influential customers who had come to what was being billed as a five-star resort, and were experiencing instead one-star service. I read the mission statement, which was vague and uninspiring. I felt there was hope, however, because one of their core intentions was to "blow the customer away." As we continued to talk, the frustrated vice-president sighed and said, "We want everyone to have a five-star experience. I guess we just have to clearly define what that experience looks like."

As we finished our lunch, we ordered espresso for dessert. After a few moments the waitress returned and said, "I'm sorry, but there is no espresso available today. Our machine is broken." Having just walked past a functioning espresso machine in the coffee bar upstairs, I smiled and asked, "Could you maybe get some from upstairs?" (There is no limit to how low espresso drinkers will stoop in order to get their coffee.) She said, "I hadn't thought of that," and within minutes returned with two perfect cups of espresso, delivered from less than twenty yards away. The vice-president sighed as she stirred her coffee. "See what I mean?" she said. "We have a long way to go in training our staff."

This was a perfect example, I felt, of the difference between training someone in dealing with transactions versus transformation. This waitress clearly felt her job was to deliver items ordered from the menu. If the items were unavailable, the transaction was still complete. The customers either got what they wanted or they didn't. She had still done her job.

If, however, the waitress had understood that her job was to "blow the customer away" with unparalleled service, she would have taken the initiative to know all the resources at her disposal, and moved heaven and earth to deliver not merely a cup of coffee, but a transformed customer.

The underlying principle of this lesson is that your first and foremost task is to teach relationship building, not "dealmaking." Out of the relationships will flow that deal, and more.

The joy of writing and studying this material is that it gets to work on me as I work on it. Yesterday, for example, I picked up the phone to call a friend who has become very dear to me. I had met him and his family at the National Prayer Breakfast, and although he is a highly paid consultant to CEOs all over the country, he has never charged me a dime for his many phone calls and support. To my knowledge, I have never given him anything measurable in dollars, either, other than perhaps some clarity on his mission statement, and what has become an undying friendship. My only desire in calling him was to see how he was doing. As we discussed the various challenges facing us, what emerged was a two-hour conversation about how we might help our mutual friends and contacts. By the time the conversation was over, we had given each other invaluable leads to an entire new client base, as well as support and encouragement. In deepening a transformational relationship, I was also caused to receive multiple transactions.

On the other hand, I am still set in my "transaction" mode at times. Just now I received a request from a woman who wants to incorporate The Path and The Path for Kids into some work she is doing with at-risk children in Houston. What she was asking for was written permission. In a hurry to get on with writing this chapter, I dashed off a note giving her the legal permission, requesting also that she submit a written report of her activities. After I signed the letter and went back to my computer, I realized that I had seen this as a simple transaction, while what was behind it was a woman doing incredible work in transformation. I made a mental note to follow up the letter with a phone call later, to see how and what she was doing.

Jesus sought and taught transformations, not transactions. When he said, "I will be with you always," he was stating his intent for lifelong follow-up on a simple exchange: "You give me your life. I give you mine." To the people who came to him, he always gave them even more than what they wanted. And he taught his team to do the same.

Jesus taught transformation, not transaction.

Questions

1. Are you teaching your team how to do transactions? What transactions are your team expected to do on a daily basis?

2. What are the possible transformations that could occur in the course of these transactions? Name five.

3. What would the result be if your team aimed at the transformation behind each transaction, rather than at the transaction itself?

4. How long did it take Jesus, in real time, to have the transformational exchange with the woman at the well? Read the entire passage of John 4:1–28 and time it.

5. How long is the average interaction between your staff and your customers?

6. Are you afraid that transformations take too long and distracts people from the real business at hand?

7. What did it cost Jesus to recruit a valuable team member, in terms of dollars and cents?

8. Have a group discussion with your team about this chapter. Identify five new things you can each and all do to create transformational experiences for your customers.

Dear Lord,
Help me to understand that transformation is possible in even
in the simplest of transactions — whether it is helping someone
get a drink of water, serve dinner, or open a door. Help me
inspire my team to go for the transformation and not the
transaction in every encounter they have. May we do it all in a
way that honors and exemplifies you.

Amen

He Turned the Pyramid
Into a Circle

In all truth I tell you, anything you ask from the
Father he will grant you in my name.
— JOHN 16:23

WORKERS AT ROADWAY EXPRESS'S bulk shipping terminal in Akron, Ohio, were amazed when they saw a music system being installed on the dock.

Being able to listen to music while they worked was an idea that the workers themselves had suggested. And it was implemented. James Stanley, president of the company, says, "In order to compete in an industry that has 5-percent net profit margins, we need to realize that every one of our 25,000 employees must be a leader." He continued, "Future opportunities are going to come from *our* people being more involved in the business."

Stanley, like so many teambuilders, is changing the hierarchical model from a pyramid to a circle. Turning the hierarchy on its ear was also evidenced by changes that took place recently at the corporate office tower of Nestlé USA. John Breen at *Fast Company* magazine reported, "Early this year, workers could be seen rolling up Oriental rugs and removing mahogany desks from what had been the company's executive suites. They were making way for employee meeting rooms and for temporary offices to be used by telecommuters. Weller and other top executives moved their offices down several floors, in part so that they could work alongside people in the trenches."

In the book *Emergence: The Connected Lives of Ants, Brains, Cities, and Software,* author Steven Johnson writes that intelligence resides at the street level of all emergent systems, whether you are talking about harvester ants or workers in the Digital Age.

Jesus redefined authority in virtually everything he did. When he turned the money changers' tables upside down, he was taking money off the top of the table in the temple, and putting it on the bottom. When he defied the ban on speaking to foreign women, by conversing with and healing the Samaritan woman, he was redefining the authority of ancient written traditions, which had become crusty and stale, and substituting in their place a new authority based on kindness and compassion.

In fact, one reason Jesus was killed was that he was changing the pyramid of well-defined ancient traditions, and turning them into a circle, with no edges or corners. That made people very uncomfortable, especially those who had risen to the top of the pyramid by virtue of their wealth or birth.

In Christianity we are told that all power rests in the Trinity, which we name as the Father, the Son, and the Holy Spirit. My sixth-grade Sunday-school teacher used to draw a picture of a triangle, and say, "God is at the top, Jesus is on one side, and the Holy Spirit is on the other."

So, in such statements as "God always does what I ask him to do," Jesus is saying that God is letting Jesus be in charge, or "on top." Then, when Jesus said, "I always do what God asks me to do," he was putting God in charge (or "on top"). When he told the disciples to wait for the Holy Spirit to come and teach them what they must do, he was putting the Holy Spirit in charge (or "on top"). A verse in the book of Wisdom in the Jerusalem Bible states that "Wisdom makes the choice of what God is to do." Someone trying to follow the flow chart of power might have a hard time asking, "Just who is in charge here?" The Trinity's answer is "We all are." That is the mystery of the Three in One. And in my mind, that can only be drawn as a circle, not as a pyramid.

It is only those teams that operate on the three-in-one principle that will succeed. Pyramids hold dead bones, and now serve only as tourist attractions. But circles! Ah, circles move quickly and envelop everyone and can grow as they add numbers without diminishing power.

As I sit here writing this, I am in the lobby of the Atlantis Paradise resort in the Bahamas. Over to my left and outside the magnificent windows is the "Mayan Pyramid" slide. Qualified "key holding" people climb six stories to the top of the tower and then plunge down a nearly vertical drop of sixty feet, into a pool of swimming sharks (that are fortunately kept away by plastic tunnels). The scene reminds me a bit of corporate America. All these people winding slowly up the stairs, only to reach the top and then slide quickly down. Because once you reach the top, where else is there to go?

Draw a triangle right here. This is the typical picture of power, of success, of wealth. The broad line at the bottom consists of the lower-class grunge workers. The two sides ascending to the top are the rising management stars. The CEO or president sits precariously at the top, trying to keep from getting skewered by what he or she knows is the very sharp and narrow point. The only way to effect change in this model is for enough people on the bottom level to get agitated enough to move up one side or the other of the triangle, causing it to topple over. Then, however, you have a new power elite at the top, and yet another set of lower-class people on the bottom.

This form of change is common in revolutions, coups, and large corporations. A militant soldier, dressed in camouflage gear and speaking for the common people, rises up one of the sides of the pyramid, using the might of the people below him. Once he gets to the top, by either killing or exiling or firing his political enemies, he becomes a new kind of dictator, often worse than the one that the people wanted him to overthrow in the first place. "Rats!" shout the wounded and disappointed people at the bottom. "Now we have to start all over again." "Progress" like this is slow.

What the Jews were hoping for in their Messiah was someone who would overthrow the Romans, so they could be in power for a change. And then here comes Jesus, saying, "The first of you must be the least. . . . If someone slaps you, turn the other cheek. . . . My kingdom is not of this world." And he added, "Those of you in power are using your priestly robes to rob and deceive. You aren't from God—you are from the Devil!" This also did not sit well with the people at the top of the religious pyramid.

When the Holy Spirit came down on the apostles gathered in the Upper Room, it fell *equally* on all the people who had gathered in prayer—it did not go from one chosen person to another in a lateral move.

"When the day of Pentecost came, *all* the believers were gathered together in one place. Suddenly there was a noise from the sky, which sounded like a strong wind blowing, and it filled the whole house where they were sitting. Then they saw what looked like tongues of fire that spread out and touched each person there. They were *all* filled with the Holy Spirit and began to talk in other languages, as the Spirit enabled them to speak" (Acts 2:1–4, emphasis supplied).

Thus the pyramid of power was suddenly transformed into a circle of flames. What happened next?

"Many miracles and wonders were done, and everyone was filled with awe. . . . And every day the Lord added to their group those who were being saved" (Acts 2:43, 47).

So, how does this relate to your team at work or at home? The truly powerful teambuilder understands that power must fall from on high, on all equally, for anything of worth to be accomplished. Intel chairman Craig Barrett observes that "the Internet has changed our culture. Now everybody has to know what everybody else is doing."

Elijah the prophet spoke about seeing "a wheel within a wheel." If each person on your team feels empowered enough to take charge when it is needed, this is having "a wheel within a wheel." If your team members are caught waiting for orders or looking for someone else to tell them what to do, then they have not been infused with the proper spirit — the one that enables them to speak in whatever language is necessary for the situation.

Nordstrom's teaches its team members to "follow your best judgment." Sales associates in each department have full authority to act on a customer's behalf, issuing no-questions-asked refunds, for example. Go into almost any retail establishment and you can tell whether it is run by a pyramid or a circle. You can immediately sense the difference.

Author John Ellis writes, "It is no accident that the killer Internet applications are e-mail and instant messaging. Both are, in practice if not technically fact, peer-to-peer technologies."

Jesus gave new meaning to peer-to-peer technology when he said, "If you ask the Father anything in my name, it will be done for you."

Jesus turned the pyramid into a circle.

Questions

1. Is the shape of your team a pyramid or a circle?
2. Do you trust your team members to act with certainty, clarity, and authority in any situation? If not, why not?
3. How much letting-go is required for you to move your team forward?
4. How can you instill a circle mentality in your team?
5. When will you recognize the circle you are in?

Prayer

Dear Lord,
You have invited me into your circle of power. Help me to invite others.

Amen

HE PRACTICED THE RULE

OF SEVEN

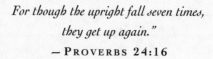

For though the upright fall seven times,
they get up again."
— **PROVERBS 24:16**

SEVEN IS CONSIDERED A special number by many. While to those rolling dice in Las Vegas it may signify a lucky win, in ancient scripture seven was considered a number with holy implications and power. According to Genesis, the world was created in six days, with God resting on the seventh. Jacob served seven years to earn the hand of Rachel. Egypt had seven years of plenty, followed by seven years of famine. In Leviticus, the priests are told to sprinkle the blood of the offering seven times before the Lord, in front of the veil of the Tabernacle (Leviticus 4:17). Joshua was told to march around the city of Jericho seven times, with seven priests bearing seven trumpets, whose blasts made the walls of the city fall.

Elisha instructed Naaman to wash in the Jordan seven times in order to be healed of his leprosy. In Psalms 119:164, David sang, "Seven times a day do I praise thee!" In Proverbs 9:1 we are told that "Wisdom . . . hath hewn out her seven pillars."

"For though the upright fall seven times, they get up again," observes Proverbs 24:16.

Jesus told his followers that "if someone sins against you seven times in one day, and seven times in a day returns to you, saying, 'I repent,' you shall forgive him."

It was seven loaves that Jesus took, blessed, and broke, to multiply into enough food to feed five thousand people.

In fact, scripture has more than seven hundred distinct references to passages with "seven" in it. According to the Women's Study Bible, King James Version, the number seven represents completeness or wholeness.

I read somewhere once that the number one represents God, the Divine.

The number three represents the Trinity. The number six represents humanity in the flesh. (Hence the significance of the number 666 representing the Antichrist, which is humanity posing as the Trinity.) And seven represents Christ, in that it is one, the Divine, plus six, humanity, or "the word becoming flesh, and dwelling among us." Completion. I am by no means advocating the pursuit of numerology in management, but I do believe that if teams practiced the rule of seven, success would be imminent. For example, working six days and resting one. It is the lack of a true Sabbath rest that is causing so much exhaustion, and thus tension and error, in the workplace.

I also think that practicing the rule of seven indicates the benefits of persistence. If Naaman had washed only four times in the Jordan, and then said, "Aw, this isn't working—forget it," he would not have been healed. While the story of the person sinning against you seven times a day, and repenting seven times a day, might strike you as being a pitiful case of a nonlearner, Jesus tells us that we must match each request for forgiveness with forgiveness, thus completing the transaction.

Ken Blanchard and Sheldon Bowles tell a wonderful story in their book *Big Bucks*, about a foreman who hands a new worker a sledgehammer and tells him to break apart a concrete slab. The worker bashes away for several minutes, knocking off only a few chips. He then admits to the foreman that apparently he is not strong enough for the job. The foreman, a small man, takes the sledgehammer from the worker and whacks a few more times against the slab. Suddenly it breaks in two. The worker then thanks him for breaking it. The foreman says, "You broke it. It just hadn't come apart yet. You'll find it best, if you want to break something, to keep hitting it until it comes apart."

Seven means diligence. Seven means faith. Seven means persistence. Seven means completion. Teambuilders need to ensure that team members do not give up on the third or fourth try.

In advertising, I learned that a person has to see your message an average of seven times before he or she "gets it." In networking I was once told to try to collect at least seven business cards at a function, making seven potential new friends. So I can't help wondering how our workplaces would change if we started to implement the rule of seven.

"We will contact a customer at least seven times in order to get our message across. We will realize that the seven customers we have are enough to build our company on. We will forgive each other at least seven times a day. We will attack this problem seven times if that is what it takes for the resistance to crumble. We will understand that with Christ in us, all things are possible, because one plus six equals seven."

"He asked them, How many loaves have you? And they said to him, seven. And then he took the seven loaves, and after giving thanks he broke them, and began handing them to his disciples to distribute; and they distributed them among the crowd. . . . They all ate as much as they wanted, and they collected seven basketfuls of the scraps left over" (Mark 8:5–8).

Jesus practiced the rule of seven.

Questions

1. Where in your work situation could you begin to practice the rule of seven?
2. Where have you been falling short?
3. What would you do if you knew that Christ was truly in you and among you?
4. Would you consider this equation true, or false: six plus one equals more than enough?

Prayer

Dear Lord,
Please forgive me my lethargy, my quickness to walk away after I've tried one or two times. Help me and my team to see our projects through to completion, even if that means we have to get into the muddy water seven times before it happens.

Amen

He Kept Them Informed

New things I do declare.

—ISAIAH 42:9

WHEN I CONDUCTED AN informal survey among management teams who worked for such companies as IBM, DeLoitte & Touche, and other large firms, I asked them what were some of the main reasons employees were leaving. The consensus led almost invariably to two factors: one was that the employees who left didn't feel "cared about," and the second was that they felt like they were being kept "out of the loop" of key information.

Jesus constantly gave his team new and exciting information, and even talked about the merchant who brings out treasures from the storehouse, some of which are old, but some of which are very new.

In Revelation 21:5 we are given a powerful image of authority and leadership. "And now the one who sits on the throne will make all things new."

Every time Jesus said "It has been written, but I say . . ." he was giving his team a new piece of information that was going to change the way things were. It was partly this constant sense of excitement that helped keep his team so motivated. They truly felt they were on the cutting edge of change, and that was right where they wanted to be.

Inc. magazine recently addressed the problem of employee turnover with a story about Barr-Nunn Transportation, a company that employs numerous truck drivers in serving customers' transportation needs. Barr-Nunn had a 55 percent turnover annually, and low morale among its team members, many of whom had little direct contact with the office. To help combat this problem, the management team at Barr-Nunn started an audiocassette newsletter — filled with four hours of industry news, interviews, company information, and a little country music. As soon as these cassette newsletters went out to its field staff, turnover dropped to 35 percent. The only thing that had changed was that the field staff suddenly felt as if they were "in the loop" again, getting new and vital information that would help them in their job delivery and, more important, help keep them connected to the team at home base.

Dr. Redmond Burke, chief of cardiovascular surgery at Miami Children's Hospital, is passionate about keeping the medical staff informed about their infants' health status. Using PDAs (personal digital assistants) now enables doctors and nurses to enter their patients' vital stats and other information several times a day. This information is automatically fed to the hospital's central database. The result is a real-time view of each patient's condition, which helps staff and parents keep current on vital information.

Among the wealthiest people in the world — Bill Gates of Microsoft and Larry Ellison of Oracle, for example — are those who are designing ways to help masses of people get and manage new information. All the fiberoptics and satellite dishes and software designers are being put in place purely for one function: to deliver information. The team leader who makes it a priority to see that his or her team is kept current not only on industry news but also on what is happening in management's thinking is the one who will have a team that runs into the huddle rather than wandering away from it—thinking it can get better information on its own.

Intel has a system that allows any new employee who joins the company to access the company's secure intranet *the day that they are hired.*

Texas Health Resources CEO Doug Hawthorne has a hotline with the call number "Yo, Doug!" to keep the fifteen thousand employees informed and up to date. Doug is also a notorious "hall walker," visiting each of his eighteen facilities on a regular schedule to keep team members "in the loop."

A Jewish official came to Jesus, knelt down before him, and said, "My daughter has just died; but come and lay your hands on her and she will live." Then Jesus went into the official's house. When he saw the musicians for the funeral and the people all stirred up, he said, "Get out, everybody. This little girl is not dead—she is only sleeping!" Then they all started making fun of him. But as soon as the people had been put out, Jesus went into the girl's room and took hold of her hand, and she got up. "The news about this spread all over that part of the country" (Matthew 9:18–26).

When Jesus told the crowd the girl wasn't dead, but sleeping, he was not just predicting a turnaround in her condition, but giving them new information.

Jesus gave them new information.

Questions

1. What new information are you providing your team?
2. Where are you getting *your* information?

3. List three examples of new information you have given your team recently. What was their response?

> ### *Prayer*
>
> *Dear Lord,*
> *Let me be a conduit of new information to my team, so that*
> *they may see you work in all your glory.*
>
> *Amen*

HE SHOWED THEM WHAT
A GOOD DAY WAS LIKE

And the word became flesh and dwelt among us.
— JOHN 1:14

BEFORE PETER MET JESUS, he probably never really had a good day. Before Mary Magdalene met Jesus, neither did she. Oh, they might have had their moments before that, but once they entered the life space of the Master, their definition of what a good day was like was totally transformed.

Jesus, through his actions, embodied what a good day in heaven was like. "And the word became flesh and dwelt among us" is one of the most powerful examples of team training ever written. I will never forget sitting at the table with the Prat family and my little godson Jacob. He was just approaching two at the time. At one point Jacob reached out for the saltshaker. We all recognized that this was the first time he was going to both pick up the implement and then salt his own food. As he happily munched on a piece of broccoli, he grabbed the saltshaker in his right hand, lifted it the appropriate height from his plate, tilted it at an angle just so, and used his pinkie finger to tap it perfectly twice.

We all burst into laughter and delight at his sophisticated learning and observation skills. No one had said, "Jacob, you tap the saltshaker twice with your little finger." He picked it up on his own. He saw the lesson in action and incorporated it into his memory bank. He had been shown what a good shake of salt looked like many times before he actually did it. That is learning at its highest and deepest — by seeing and then doing. That is how Jesus taught — not so much with his words as with his deeds.

Fast Company magazine writer John Ellis summarized this principle when he said leaders show that "many things matter, and here's what matters most."

You are right now demonstrating to your team what a good day is by your actions. When the administration of the Catholic Health Care East annual meeting shows a picture of one of their physicians kneeling to help a homeless man in the street, they are teaching their team workers "This is a good day." When parents take their kids to a child crisis center to give away some of their toys, they are showing children what a good day is like. When CEOs stop to inquire about the health of a janitor's mother, they are showing what a good day is like.

Oh, the responsibility that awaits us as we demonstrate, through our actions to our team, what a good day is.

Each of us must define and examine what makes a good day for us. And then we need to recognize that that message will be replicated a hundredfold by those whom we lead, down to the last detail — like two finger taps on a saltshaker.

Jesus showed them what a good day was like.

Questions

1. What is a good day for you? Write it down. Include at least seven different elements or actions that it would include.
2. How close are you to living that now?
3. What would Jesus think about your day?

4. Where do you see your team mimicking your behavior — even in subtle and unconscious ways?

5. What activities can you add, revise, or delete to make your good day even better?

6. What will be the impact on your team if and when you start *really* living good days?

Prayer

Dear Lord,
You showed us all what a good day would include. Let me ever see you as my example.

Amen

He Rewarded Assertiveness

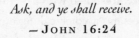

Ask, and ye shall receive.

— JOHN 16:24

EVERY CATALOG I GET from the American Management Association mentions *assertiveness* in course offerings.

To assert oneself means "to put oneself forward boldly or forcefully." While employees rank two-way communication second only to salary as very important to job satisfaction, according to John Izzo and Pam Withers in their book *Values Shift*, seven out of ten workers rarely, if ever, share their requests or opinions with top management. Clearly, teambuilders need to teach and reward assertiveness.

The word *ask* and its derivatives appear more than three hundred times in scriptures. It was a primary, fundamental teaching of Jesus: "*Ask*, and ye shall receive." "Whatsoever you *ask* in my name, shall be given to you." "Would you *ask* your father for a fish and receive a stone?"

He rewarded three very assertive women in a time and culture where "pushy women" were frowned upon if not downright forbidden. It was an assertive woman, his mother, Mary, who got Jesus to perform his first miracle (John 2:1–11). An assertive woman daring to touch Jesus' garment was healed, even after violating a long-standing taboo (Matthew 9:20–22). A persistent widow, refusing to be ignored by a lazy, sleeping judge, was eventually granted her wish (Luke 18:1–8). Jesus, humble as he was, urged people, and women especially, to be bold in their requests.

Although Paul didn't want women to be allowed to speak in church, Jesus urged women to speak up and out — often. In fact, in the book of Proverbs and in the apocryphal Wisdom (the *New Jerusalem Bible*), we are presented with a picture of wisdom as both a feminine intelligence and a voice calling out from the city gates to anyone who will listen. "Listen! Wisdom is calling out. Reason is making herself heard. On the hilltops near the road and at the crossroads she stands. I call to everyone on Earth — listen to my excellent words" (Proverbs 8:1–6).

In another beautiful passage we are told that "wisdom makes choice of the works God is to do" (Wisdom 8:4).

In her book *Play Like a Man, Win Like a Woman,* Gail Evans writes that all too often women tend to live in the complaint rather than asking clearly for what they want and need. She says that we often expect others to read our minds, pick up on our cleverly dropped hints, or accurately interpret our sighs and raised eyebrows.

A female phenomenon I have observed is that of preceding requests with apologies. "I'm sorry to disturb you, but could you pass me the ketchup" seems polite, but I've also heard twelve-year-old girls saying "I'm sorry" far more often than their male counterparts. If you start out being sorry, where do you go from there?

Jesus didn't pray, "Dear Lord, I'm sorry to disturb you, but could you please raise Lazarus?"

When Jesus raised the little girl from death, he didn't say, "I'm sorry, but could you all please leave the room *so I can do some work in here?*"

All of us, male and female, must learn to call upon our divine rank and privilege with confidence, not shame. A recent study of top leaders found that their assertiveness was tempered with kindness and fairness — not with aggressive demands. As team leaders we must learn to ask clearly, ask often, and ask confidently.

Jesus taught assertiveness.

Questions

1. What do you need to ask for, but feel afraid to do so?
2. How clearly and confidently do you ask?
3. What is being lost by you and your team's lack of assertiveness?

Prayer

Dear Lord,

You taught your disciples to ask confidently, assertively, and often for their daily bread, as well as for forgiveness, which would clear the way for your loving power to pour into and through them. Help me learn to do the same.

Amen

He Was Kind, but Not

Always Nice

I have come not to bring peace, but a sword.
— MATTHEW 10:34

D O YOU THINK JESUS was nice? Recently I was being interviewed for a magazine article. The interviewer asked, "Laurie, would you say you are a nice person?" "Frequently, but not always," I answered. His eyebrows shot up as if he'd discovered a blot on my soul. "You're not nice?" he exclaimed. I smiled and reiterated that mostly I was, but not always.

But then again, neither was Jesus. Was Jesus nice to the scribes and Pharisees, or the money changers in the temple? Was Joan of Arc nice when she defied the bishop and insisted that she had indeed heard those voices? Christians in general, and women and girls especially, are always supposed to be "nice," but there is a difference between being nice and being kind. *Nice,* according to the dictionary, means pleasing, agreeable, or courteous. *Kind* means showing sympathy or understanding.

Is a mother bear nice when she defends her cubs? Is a mare nice when she kicks her newborn colt with the front of her hoof, urging it to get up *now?* Parents learn very quickly the distinction between being nice and being kind. Were the Allied leaders who divided up Czechoslovakia and gave it to Hitler being "nice" to him? Is a woman who consoles her sobbing husband after he's beaten her black and blue being "nice" to him?

As team leaders we must not confuse being kind with being nice, or we will lead the team to its detriment. My study of leaders reveals that they must be willing to stand two things we all usually want to avoid at all costs: rejection and confrontation. Where is the "niceness" in those?

A friend of mine who is a dedicated servant of God was being interviewed for a position she very much wanted. The committee had looked up and interviewed two of the people she'd had to fire over the last twenty years. The elderly deacon looked at her and said, "You know, we can't build a church on a string of broken hearts." As she was sharing this story with me, I said, "You should have told that deacon to reread the Gospel."

"And the angel looked at Mary and said, 'He will be a shining light unto Israel, but his sword will pierce your soul.'"

Jesus looked at the man who wanted to follow him *after* he'd taken the time to bury his father, and said, "Let the dead bury the dead."

Jesus said, "Unless you hate your natural family enough to follow me, you are not worthy of me."

Jesus said, "I have come to bring not peace, but a sword."

Mary said, "Lord, if you'd been here sooner, Lazarus would not have died."

Now picture that deacon interviewing a young Jesus. "You know, Jesus, you cannot build your work on a string of broken hearts."

And Jesus looks at him and says, "I must do what my Father tells me to do, no matter who it upsets."

Leaders would do well to recognize the difference between being nice and being kind.

Jesus was kind, but not always nice.

Questions

1. Are you a nice person?
2. What is the difference between being nice and being kind?
3. Why, and when, could it be dangerous to cultivate a culture of "niceness" in your team?
4. What are some examples you — and your team — might give of occasions when being nice is actually being cowardly, self-sabotaging, unserving, or duplicitous?

Prayer

Dear Lord,
You were one of the kindest people who ever lived, but you did not fear or avoid confrontation just to win the "nice" award. Help me and my team to do and be the same.

Amen

He Went Deep in Order
to Go Wide

And soon it was a river that I could not pass through.
— Ezekiel 47:5

The Persian poet Rumi says, "You must always carry an unsolvable problem in your heart."

When Steve Jobs and Steve Wosniak went into their garage, their unsolvable problem was "How do we make computerized intelligence available to the everyday person?" Apple was born.

When Phil Knight sat down with some rubber and a waffle iron, his unsolvable problem was "How do we make shoes that help cushion the human anatomy?" Nike was born.

When God asked, "How can I get my people to come back to me?" Jesus was born.

It is when we are willing to carry the unsolvable problem in our hearts that innovation and creativity is born. And in order to solve the unsolvable problem, we must be willing to go deep, for if the answers were on the surface, we would have found them by now. Unfortunately, we live in a world that teaches us to go shallow.

Going deep means being willing to drop the boundaries of your conscious, knowing mind and enter into the silence of that which is already Known.

This is the deepest prayer —

> *When you wait for the answers . . .*
> *when you simply*
> *wait . . .*
> *and as you wait the answer*
> *comes into you*
> *and through you,*
> *if you will.*

And as you rise, you realize that somehow you are part of the answer.

I have always been challenged by the concept of meditation. After studying it and realizing that so much of my prayer is a one-way dialogue of directive conversation, I decided recently to accept the invitation of a friend to experience the sheer silence of meditation — undirected prayer.

As I went below my "Hello, God," "Thank you, God," and "Please, God," I found myself being able to be at peace, of peace. Without trying to go anywhere with it, or get anything out of it, I felt that my heart was beating at the same rate as God's. It was a few moments of bliss, of escape, of knowing that I am known.

And I realized just a taste of what the saints and mystics and certainly Jesus must have experienced. I realized in those moments that I already had all the "results" I was seeking — the sense of unity with God.

In Jesus' prayer "that they may be one, Father, even as you and I are one," I had before only sensed intellectually what he was saying. But by going deep into prayer I could almost feel it. I had often wondered how, for example, the saints and martyrs could so effortlessly let go of their possessions.

> *When you realize you are one with God's love,*
> *why would you need earthly possessions?*

True Christianity stems ultimately from being "in the vine," not from following an externally imposed set of rules and restrictions. Goodness becomes the *natural* order of things when we go deep in Christ, when we enter into the Holy of Holiness that is prayer.

We no longer need to stand at the door and knock.
We now dwell in the castle.

We no longer need to build up our bank accounts.
We are heirs to the Royal Treasury.

Jesus, Teambuilder, went often and alone to pray. Jesus went deep in order to go wide.

Questions

1. Do you go deep, or merely shallow?
2. What is beyond your directive, "Do this, don't do that, God" prayers?
3. What if you could *be* there, with and in God all the time?
4. How might your team's performance improve if you went deep more often?

Prayer

Dear Lord,
Help me be the answer to the unsolvable problem — if only through my willingness and ability to go deep in you. Help my team also carry an unsolvable problem, for the problem they choose will effect its answer through and upon them. Help us be one, as you are one.

Amen

He Identified Coachable

Moments

Do you want to be healed?
— John 5:6

O ne of the fastest-growing movements in the country is personal coaching. Whereas in the past coaching was limited to the ranks of athletes, now everyone either has or wants a coach, or mentor.

When you look at how Jesus trained his team, it was not through a highly polished, spiral-bound, or even Power Point presentation. It was through a three-year series of individual "coachable moments." Any teacher can tell you that you cannot teach a student who does not want to learn, and Jesus certainly encountered his share of those. But he knew, and was trained to identify, those moments in people's lives when their hearts and minds were open to learn new ways of relating to the world.

Fast Company magazine recently profiled a mentorship relationship between two CEOs. One CEO who agreed to be a mentor to a young, rising executive shared that "in a boardroom setting, you are one of seven to ten people" addressing a situation. As a mentor and coach, he said, he found tremendous personal satisfaction in seeing someone learn a valuable new skill set. The question one asks himself as a coach and mentor is "How can I train this person to be even more of a winner?" (In *Fast Company* magazine, January 2001.)

Olympic coaches use video replays of team members' performances, both good and bad, to help athletes modify, improve, and at times repeat their behaviors. These "stop and pause" portions of training are "coachable moments."

When I ask people on a regular basis what they would really like to be doing with their lives, overwhelmingly the answer comes back, "I think I'd like to become a personal coach." We seem to have this innate desire to want to help others, and coaching on a one-to-one level is a tremendous way to meet that need.

The International Coaching Federation, for example, has grown in three years from a mere handful of members to more than ten thousand worldwide.

So you want to be a coach? Well, then, you have to learn to identify "coachable moments" or all your work is for naught (or "knot," as stress managers like to say).

Lieutenant Colonel Scott Snook heads the Office of Policy, Planning and Analysis for West Point, with a mandate to update their leadership development programs. "Cadets at West Point advance by resolving competing claims on their identity, and by encountering experiences in which they sometimes fail. Sometimes, the biggest window for changing someone's self-concept opens when he or she fails." (In *Fast Company* magazine, July 2001.)

Coachable moments come only at points of vulnerability, humility, hunger, fear, and need. For example, the adulterous woman about to be stoned to death was vulnerable, humbled, fearful, and in need. Jesus identified the coachable moment for her, and said, "Go and sin no more."

As the crowds departed after hearing some of Jesus's challenging statements, Jesus, rather than feel himself a failure, turned it into a coachable moment for his own staff, asking them, "Do you also want to leave?" Teambuilders recognize the opportunity for coaching even in moments of what look like personal crisis.

When the crowds were gathered on a beautiful hillside overlooking an azure sea, Jesus seized a magnificent coachable moment and spoke out the Beatitudes, a series of teachings so simple yet so profound that many people can recite them by memory some two thousand years later.

When the Roman guards were mocking him and hitting him and spitting on him, Jesus said not a word. This was, sadly, *not* a coachable moment in these young men's lives.

A coach must know not only *what* to teach, but, perhaps more important, *when*. This is what makes a coach a coach rather than, say, a *boss*. "One man had an illness which had lasted thirty-eight years, and when Jesus saw him lying there and knew that he had been in that condition a long time, he said, 'Do you want to be well again?'" (John 5:5–6).

Jesus identified coachable moments.

Questions

1. Can you identify some coachable moments in your life when you were really (finally) ready to learn?
2. Think back on a recent coachable moment you experienced with a member of your team. What were the circumstances?
3. How can you, as a coach, be poised for coachable moments when they come?
4. What is the difference between a coach and a boss?

Prayer

Dear Lord,
Be my coach. Walk with me daily, and identify the coachable
moments in me. In fact, make my entire mindset that of being
"coachable," and please grant my team the same.

Amen

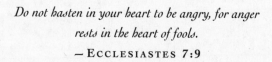

*Do not hasten in your heart to be angry, for anger
rests in the heart of fools.*
— Ecclesiastes 7:9

I DON'T FIGHT EVERY battle I see. I can't. And neither can you. I have determined, after many trials, that my best weapon is not my mouth but my pen — and my battlefield is the blank page. And every day I think about Jesus, and the fact that he, too, had to choose his battles.

Imagine how he must have felt when he saw a Roman soldier hit a Jew, or watched people spit on prostitutes, or walked past the crucified people dying alongside the road. Jesus was not the first person to be crucified in Jerusalem. This horror was a regular occurrence. Yet there is no record of Jesus leading any protest marches to overthrow Roman tyranny or halt the execution of others. Why not? Didn't he care?

Of course he cared. But Jesus was wise enough to choose his battles, to save his energy for the one battle he could win, the one that would change history — not because he picked up his sword, but because he laid down his life.

As a new (very new) student of the discipline that is t'ai chi, I have been fascinated to learn that when the body doesn't seem to be doing anything outwardly, that is when the most intense inner discipline is taking place. As a person who loves to chase balls around a racquetball court in order to work up a good sweat, I always scoffed at those slow-moving people I'd see hovering like one-legged cranes in the park. Now that I have done t'ai chi, I know that getting the body and mind and spirit perfectly balanced and poised is no small feat. And never have I felt more inner physical power than when I stood perfectly balanced, perfectly still, and "understood my place in the ocean." Sally McLaughlin, the woman who taught my first class, says the study of t'ai chi takes years of mental discipline — but those who master it can stand perfectly still, and crush a rock in their bare hands.

Balance. Poise. Knowing your place. Knowing how and where best to apply pressure, and maintain grace and dignity while doing so. Now — that is power. That is leverage. That is the very fine art of knowing exactly what business you're in — and trying to do no other.

Michael Saylor, the young, formerly bullish CEO of Micro-Strategy, Inc., was chastened as he watched his company's stock price drop from $226.75 a share to $86.75 a share in one day. He personally lost $6.1 billion in paper wealth, becoming one of the poster boys of the tech economy's rise and fall. He attributes his fall in part to arrogance, stating in a *Fast Company* magazine interview that "we put all of our energy into promotionalism rather than operational excellence. There was no problem that we thought we couldn't tackle."

Now, however, Saylor is content for his company to focus on its forte: making software that analyzes a company's database and identifies trends that can cut costs and boost revenues. Saylor and his team have learned to choose their battles.

Jesus knew exactly what business he was in when he said, "My Kingdom is not of this world," and refused to be drawn into political debates. Could he have crushed the Romans? Absolutely. Could he have thrown off the tyranny of Caesar? Without a doubt. Then why didn't he? Because it was literally none of his business. He came here to complete one task, and that's the one he completed. That is also obedience. And complete trust.

So many teams scatter their energy because they forget what business they're in. They try to take up battles that are not theirs. They try to be all things to all people, and thus lose their saltiness. In fact, every teambuilder would be wise to remind the team daily what business they are really in.

Jesus chose his battles carefully. And his battles always had to do with winning the human heart — one heart at a time.

Jesus chose his battles.

Questions

1. What battles have you been fighting?
2. What business are you really in?
3. What business is your team really in?
4. How could the philosophy of winning "one heart at a time" be applied to your team's situation?
5. What might be the result if this were the "battle" you really engaged in, and to which you gave yourself wholeheartedly?

Prayer

Dear Lord,
You didn't chase after every rabbit that crossed your path. You
didn't try to right every wrong or win every war or beat the bad
guys into submission. You gave yourself over totally to being
love, to teaching love — one heart at a time — and the world was
changed. Blessed be your energy, your discipline. So may mine
always be focused on you.

Amen

He Didn't Smash the Gnat

and Lose the Camel

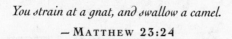

You strain at a gnat, and swallow a camel.
— Matthew 23:24

A FRIEND OF MINE who is a very successful author shared a valuable lesson with me. He was attending a business conference at which he was also to be a speaker, and noticed that one of the other speakers had "plagiarized" one of his quotes. "I couldn't believe it!" he said. "There were my exact words on his 'six points of life' slides. He was using one of my quotes as if it were his own idea — taken from his life experience." "What did you do?" I asked him. "My first reaction was to go up to him after the conference and demand that he give proper attribution. I even thought about calling my attorney. But then I decided to take a day and cool off. After all, is there really anything new under the sun? And besides, I thought to myself, maybe I should be flattered that this principle I asserted in my book is becoming common knowledge. Still, it stung a little bit, and I prayed about what to do.

"The next day I ran into this guy in the hall, and forced myself to be nice to him. He had, after all, said he gave a copy of my books to all his clients, and he had some pretty big-name clients. Then I learned that his mother had just died, and that really hit me hard. I am blessed enough to still have my mother living, and I could only imagine what a loss that must be.

"So you decided just to let it go?" I asked incredulously, knowing this man to be quite competitive and assertive.

"I was going to. But then I ran into him again in the steam room. I thought about how instead of hurting this guy, maybe I could help him. After all, the fact that he liked my book and agreed with some of my stuff, even enough to copy it, meant that at some level we had similar values. So as I was sitting there literally getting steamed, I found myself asking him how I could serve him and his company. Oddly enough, the minute I asked him that question, I found all my anger disappear."

"What happened then?" I asked.

"We started talking, and the more we talked, the more we realized that we might be able to do some strategic partnering in key markets. We're having breakfast in the morning to discuss how I can build him into my business thinking, and he can build me into his."

Maybe that's what Jesus meant when he said, "When someone strikes you, don't hit them back. Turn the other cheek." Then you will be looking at them from a different perspective.

Jesus did not smash the gnat to lose the camel. In this particular instance, if my friend had gone up and demanded to be recognized as the author of the quote, he probably would have gotten his name on a measly slide. I'd be willing to bet, though, that the guy would have pulled the slide altogether and made up something to go in its place. Big deal. The annoying gnat would be smashed. But in doing that, my friend would almost certainly have lost what ultimately became a key strategic partner for him—a camel that carried his books and reputation into faraway lands and new territories—because of a kind and wise approach.

He was a much bigger man/author/consultant than this other

guy was. But he didn't try to squash him. He tried to lift him up, and in so doing he was blessed.

Teambuilders know to let the little things go, and keep their eyes always focused on what is good and true, and part of the bigger picture.

A father who swats his son with a belt twice weekly, because of a B on a report card, is squashing a gnat and losing the camel. With every swat he is driving that child farther and farther away—not from a good report card, perhaps, but definitely from him.

Teambuilders do not abuse their workers to get the work done. Jesus prided himself as a carpenter for making yokes that fit the oxen so well they never caused blisters. "Come unto me, for my yoke is easy and my burden light" (Matthew 11:30). Yet I have seen—and perhaps you have, too—bosses and managers who pick on the smallest infractions and miss the bigger issues altogether.

The Book of Proverbs warns about the miseries of living with a complaining spouse. That drip, drip, drip of excess negativity can drive anyone away. And has.

Time and again I have heard staff people say that no matter what they do right, their boss sees only the mistakes. The feeling of being not enough, demonstrated by having bosses picking at nits, is driving more people away from their jobs than you could even imagine.

Jesus did not squash the gnat, and lose the camel.

Questions

1. What problem on your team is driving you crazy right now?
2. How big, really, is it?
3. Are you going to address it by attacking, or by surrounding and uplifting?

4. Have you ever been alienated by someone whose focus always seemed to be on gnats? I know a story of a woman who lost her life because while she was driving she tried to kill a fly.

5. How can you, as a teambuilder, learn to differentiate between the gnats and the camels?

Prayer

Dear Lord,
You could always truly discern the big things from the little things — the important from the unimportant — the "heart" issues from the "mouth" issues. Help me do the same.

Amen

HE RELEASED THEM

W E SPEND SO MUCH time concentrating on building our faith in God that we often forget to think about God's faith in us.

From the very beginning, God instilled in us free will, and left us alone to give us a chance to make the right choices.

The Gospel is ultimately about release — the freedom Jesus gave us to choose and choose again.

In Dostoyevsky's *The Grand Inquisitor*, Jesus is held hostage and accused of not loving all the people, but only a few. He is told that if he'd loved all the people he would have caved in to the earlier temptation to turn stones into bread and let them *all* be fed — forever and ever, until they died. "But you turned down the bread and gave them freedom instead — thus loving only the few who have the courage to take it. *All of us* are hungry, you know, but not all of us care to be free," says the Inquisitor.

Jesus smiles and confirms his choice for free will yet again, and the Inquisitor kisses him, with a smile and a plan to feed all the rest of the people in a gilded cage so they would never leave.

Jesus spoke for radical freedom.

The ultimate test for any teambuilder is the act of release. The parents who drop their children off at school, the teachers who open the door one last time, the majors and colonels who must send their troops into the field of battle — all of these experience the pang and pain of release: "Have I done everything I could? Have I taught them well enough? Have I prepared them for every possible contingency?" These are the thoughts that ricochet through the mind as the heart melts in good-bye.

Yet not to release them would, in fact, be the ultimate betrayal. A teambuilder's job is always and finally to let go — trusting that the excitement and grounding work has been done, that the transformation is complete, that the time for release is at hand: "For I have given them the teaching that you gave me and they have indeed accepted it" (John 17:8).

Jesus released his team in many ways. He *released their genius*, and *kept the overhead low*, so they would be free to work *unencumbered*. He *made them face their unfaceables*, so their shadow side would not overwhelm them. *He made training the reward*, offering to keep them eternally excited about their work. *He shared responsibility for customer satisfaction, turning everyone into recruiters and leaders as well.*

I read again, with tears in my eyes, the following passage: "When he had said this, he cried in a loud voice Lazarus, come out! The dead man came out, his feet and hands bound with strips of material and cloth over his face. Jesus said to them 'Unbind him, and let him go free'" (John 11:43–44).

This is every teambuilder's task: to take the strips of cloth from their hands and faces, to unbind them, and let them go free.

HE TURNED EVERYONE

INTO A RECRUITER

Go therefore and make disciples of all nations.
— MATTHEW 28:19

A TEAM'S LONGEVITY DEPENDS ON its ability to recruit new talent. Every teambuilder knows that talent is the lifeblood of an organization. So where do you find it? If you're like Greg Peters, CEO of the Vignette Corporation, you turn to your own. A recent *Fast Company* magazine article reported that in less than three years Vignette went from one hundred employees to 2,300 employees worldwide. Recruiting director Stephanie Beard, who was Vignette's one hundredth hire, says, "We are looking for people who aren't looking for work," which obviously requires a whole new level of recruiting expertise. Vignette found that its greatest talent for recruiting lay in its own ranks. Vignette employees — all of them — are asked to devote 10 percent of their time to recruiting. The incentive for this effort is twofold. One is money. Every employee whose referral signs on gets a $2,000 bonus. And whoever has referred the most new hires at the end of the year gets a two-year lease on a Mercedes-Benz. The other incentive is that all employees, through stock options, are in fact owners of the company. "And we all want to bring in the most entrepreneurial, passionate people," says the CEO.

So far, more than 60 percent of Vignette's new hires come through referrals. And only 3 percent of the talent pool leaves, compared to a whopping 28 percent, which is standard in the industry. Vignette has grown through turning everyone into recruiters.

Jesus' ministry grew through the very same principles (although his incentives, like "living water," were a bit more eternal and ethereal than a two-year lease on the best-looking donkey in town).

It is interesting to note that after nearly every transaction Jesus had with a "customer," they would go and tell everyone what they had seen and heard, even on those rare occasions when he asked them not to do so.

The woman at the well ran and got all her friends. The man who had been blind from birth shouted the news of his restored vision to a whole village. Andrew the disciple went and brought others to Jesus. In fact, Jesus did not have a no-nepotism policy. He actively recruited entire families. Who knew him first, for example? Mary, Martha, or Lazarus? Regardless of who made first contact, the whole family fell in love with him. James and John whom he called the "sons of thunder," came to Jesus as a matching set. Jesus, in fact, was the son recruited by his Father, and John the Baptist was Jesus' cousin.

Michael Cardone Jr., president of Cardone Industries, an international remanufacturing firm, states, "We actively encourage nepotism in our plants. We have found that there are multiple benefits in this. One is that family members know each other's strengths and talents. The other is that since their reputation and honor is at stake, they keep a watchful eye on the family members they have recruited, making double sure that they do their job, and do it well."

I was surprised to learn recently that the turnover rate in the *maquilas* in Juarez, Mexico, is a whopping 80 percent. "We pay them good wages," said the plant manager who told me this. "They come from sometimes hundreds of miles away, attracted by the opportunities. We teach them English. We offer them health benefits. We feed them twice a day." "Then why do they leave?" I asked him. "They get homesick," he replied. In the Mexican culture, family is everything. One young worker said, "This good job is costing my heart too much." Thus, some *maquila* managers are offering family recruiting plans.

"Viral marketing" is the phenomenon that every business owner desires. That is, of course, the "sneeze effect" whereby one person infects or excites the others around him or her, and the excitement spreads exponentially at lightning speed.

Martin Rutte, coauthor of *Chicken Soup for the Soul at Work*, recently shared with me an astonishing statistic. Do you know how long it would take a message to reach every one of the 6 billion people on the planet if the only "recruiting" method was to "Tell two people, and ask those two people to tell two more." I guessed six months. The accurate answer is thirty-three days. Teambuilders know that every team depends on new talent to thrive.

"Go and tell everyone what you have seen and heard," he said. Jesus turned everyone into recruiters.

Questions

1. What does your recruiting plan look like?
2. Do you put the weight on only one person or department?
3. What tangible and intangible rewards are you offering?

Prayer

Dear Lord,
I got here because somebody took the time to tell me about your incredible plan. Help me and my team remember to do the same — and recruit others to do so, also.

Amen

HE RELEASED THEIR GENIUS

You did not choose me — I chose you.

— JOHN 15:16

GAY HENDRICKS IS A psychologist and consultant who helps individuals and corporations improve their performance. He asks clients to divide a sheet of paper into four squares. At the upper left and right corners respectively are the words "Genius" and "Excellent." The lower two quadrants are labeled "Competent" and "Incompetent." He then asks each individual to begin filling in each square with a list of their skills, talents, and work activities, putting them each in their appropriate place. For example, under "incompetent" a client might write words like "organizing," "scheduling," "attention to detail." In the "genius" quadrant that same person might write words or skills like "motivating others, seeing the big picture, generating new ideas."

The purpose of this exercise is to have people realize and admit where they shine and where they don't. It is important to note that many people are constantly trying to improve their lower two quadrants, "Competence" and "Incompetence," while making only occasional forays into their areas of pure "genius."

Teambuilders must have the ability to help their team members move into operating out of their "genius" at least 80 percent of the time. Jesus specialized in releasing the genius in others, moving his original team members from incompetence to genius again and again. Take Simon Peter, for example. Jesus saw that Peter was fairly incompetent at fishing for fish, and moved him into the area of fishing for souls. Peter went from toiling all day and catching nothing to being called, in effect, the Head Fisherman. "Upon this rock I will build my Church," Jesus said of him. Although Peter's transformation was a long, splashy, ear-slicing, and heartbreaking one, it was real, it was deep, and it was profound.

Paul was another team member (albeit a late addition) who experienced the transformation from incompetence to genius. Paul, as a zealous persecutor of Christ's followers, was incompetent at encouraging others or building them up. He specialized in tearing things down, and even admitted that he stood present and consenting at the stoning death of Stephen, the first Christian martyr.

Yet, after being knocked off his ass (literally) by a blinding light, and hearing Jesus' voice saying "Saul, Saul, why do you persecute me?" Saul — now Paul — went from being a thrower of stones to a builder of churches. His letters to young church groups in Corinth or Galatia or Ephesus helped shape a movement that was just getting started. Saul the bully became Paul the helper. He was obviously an incompetent persecutor but a genius motivator. His team leader called forth that transformation in him.

Mary Magdalene went from being faithless to being faithful. She wasn't very good at loving many men, but became legendary at loving one. She went from running from commitment to embodying it. Jesus released her genius.

A good team leader encourages his or her people to quit doing what they are bad at, and start doing what they are good at — and then move from doing what they are good at into the area where they operate at "genius" level.

If surveys reveal that at least 70 percent of workers are in the wrong job, then the teambuilder's main focus must be to get them into the right work. An executive of a large insurance firm recently shared with me the following experience:

When, based on performance reviews, it becomes obvious to him that a person isn't cutting it, he calls them into his office, usually on a Friday, and says, "This job obviously isn't suiting you. What I'd like you to think about seriously this weekend is where in this organization you think your genius could be released. Then, if you and I and your supervisor agree, we will reassign you to that department for ninety days to see if it makes a better fit."

The transformations he has seen have been amazing. In the few cases where there was absolutely no fit in any department, he called them into his office again, after meeting with them weekly during the ninety days, and pledged to use all his resources to help relocate or re-source that worker into another organization.

"In the eight years since I've been doing this," he shared, "I haven't had to fire anyone. People have been transferred into different departments, and some people have left voluntarily, but it was with the understanding that I had done my level best to help them find their genius."

A pastor I know lamented the workers he had wounded by arbitrarily putting people into "jobs," rather than helping identify and then release them into areas of greater job and effectiveness. "Finally I got it," he told me. "The person handling the church finances really wanted to be a youth pastor, and once we identified her real genius, she blossomed and so did we."

When Jesus took a stumbling man who had been begging and blind from birth and turned him into a courageous witness bold enough to testify before the Pharisees, he was demonstrating what all good teambuilders do.

Jesus released their genius.

Questions

1. Where are your team members blind to their own genius?
2. Which of your team members still believe themselves unable to walk?
3. What is the teambuilder's role in releasing genius?
4. List four things that teambuilders can do to take people from incompetence to genius.

Prayer

Dear Lord,
Help me recognize where I am blindly trying to improve my team's push-ups, when you have called me to see the truth and release the dance of genius in them.

Amen

HE SENT THEM OUT
UNENCUMBERED

He instructed them to take nothing for the journey
but a walking stick.
— MARK 6:8, *THE LEARNING BIBLE*

HAVE YOU EVER READ a book that was so funny you laughed out loud — in a public place — so loud that tears started rolling down your face? I have. I was on a plane reading Bill Bryson's book *A Walk in the Woods* when it happened. The author's images of preparing for his hike of the Appalachian Trail, and the companion who showed up to go with him, had me practically snorting in delight. A quick synopsis, if you haven't read the story, is that an out-of-shape middle-aged man decides to walk the entire length of the Appalachian Trail. He tries fruitlessly to persuade his wife or coworkers to go with him. He advertises for a companion in all the hiking magazines. Finally, in desperation, he contacts an old high school buddy, who agrees to join him.

When he goes out to meet his friend Fred at the airport, instead of a fit, tanned, athletic companion, he is greeted by a slovenly, out-of-shape character whose packing consists solely of massive amounts of Snickers bars and toilet paper.

Suffice it to say this well-thought-out journey does not go as planned; many of the most humorous happenings are caused by the overzealous and ineffectual packing skills of Bryson's companion. Only when Bill helps unencumber his poorly packed friend does the journey proceed with fewer mishaps.

If you understand that your function as a team leader is, like Jesus, to send your team out without any "baggage" to carry, you too will experience a sense of great release. Jesus' lack of a packing list showed amazing trust. First of all, he knew God would protect his team; second, he knew that the things they needed would be provided for; and, third, he knew they would meet enough of the right people on the way to make their journey successful.

Is your team enslaved to supporting your overhead, or baggage, or are they debt-free enough to serve your customers? Just as "guilty feet have no rhythm," neither do feet in mortgaged shoes. I have seen hospitals so crippled by acquisition and merger debts that the administration laid off nurses and cut patient services in order to maintain the buildings.

In a recent Medicare fraud scandal, several CEOs of hospitals were convicted of trying to cheat the government out of millions of dollars by falsifying claims. Consultants who had worked within that particular system had early on predicted bad tidings — stating that the debt load and subsequent shareholder pressure were so high that inevitably some people were going to crack in order to try to sustain it. In this case the fraud was not perpetrated by people trying to line their own pockets, but rather by people trying to keep meeting an overbearing bottom line.

Consider the impact of a big overhead (investor debt and expectations) on a creative spirit. How much does borrowed money really cost?

Doug Hawthorne, CEO of Texas Health Resources, faced a newly merged health-care conglomerate burdened with a $20-million debt. He and the board took quick measures to sell off non-performing assets, and within two years that same organization showed a $20-million profit. I was with him the day he joyously distributed profit-sharing checks to all the employees — even the janitors. He and his leadership team had helped free the team members from working hard to service a debt from the past, so they could move with confidence into the future.

Jesus sent his team out unencumbered.

Questions

1. What is the debt load of your team?
2. What resources might you be causing them to overlook by overpacking?
3. Do you have the courage to send your team out unencumbered?

Prayer

Dear Lord,
I've got my walking stick — and like Moses, I'm ready to go.
Help me teach my team to do the same.

Amen

HE KEPT IT SIMPLE

And a child shall lead them.

— ISAIAH 11:6

M Y FRIEND LISA DAHLBERG, a highly respected health-care consultant, recently sent me this e-mail quiz, which had been forwarded to her. Apparently this is a quiz that a major consulting firm gives to professionals, presumably in its interviewing process.

1. How do you put a giraffe in the refrigerator?
2. How do you put an elephant in the refrigerator?
3. The Lion King is hosting an Animal Conference. All the animals attend except one. Which one does not attend?
4. You must cross a river, but it is infested with crocodiles. How do you manage it?

Question 1 tests whether you do things in an overly complicated way. Question 2 tests your ability to think through the repercussions of your actions. Question 3 tests your memory. Question 4 tests whether you learn quickly from your mistakes.

Now for the answers:

1. The way to put a giraffe in the refrigerator is to open the refrigerator door, put in the giraffe, and then close it.
2. The way to put an elephant in the refrigerator is to open the door, take out the giraffe, put in the elephant, and then close it.
3. The animal that does not attend the Animal Conference is the elephant, because it is in the refrigerator.
4. The way to get across a river is to swim across it. It is safe because you know that all the crocodiles are attending the Lion King's Animal Conference.

According to my sources, fully 90 percent of the professionals tested missed all of the questions. However, many preschoolers gave several correct answers. Perhaps this study suggests that more professionals should approach things like a four-year-old.

Yesterday I had lunch with the CEO of our local YMCA. He was telling me of a generous couple who had donated land for a soccer field, which was on the other side of a four-foot-wide canal. The land was worth several hundred thousand dollars. But twelve different city, federal, and state organizations had to be consulted and their permission secured before a simple cement bridge, which ultimately cost more than the land it was built to reach, could be constructed over the canal.

This morning I filled out six sets of tax forms for the city of Philadelphia. I recently conducted a one-day seminar in the city, not knowing that one must purchase a business license, and send in copies of all federal tax returns, in order to do business in this fine city of our forefathers (who revolted, by the way, partly because of outrageous taxation). By the time my accountant, two lawyers, and three people on the city of Philadelphia's payroll got it all figured out, I owed them thirty-four dollars. Quick calculations on my part of the hourly rate of all the professionals involved revealed that it cost at least six thousand dollars to collect thirty-four.

If there is one group of people that Jesus really didn't like, it was not the tax collectors, however. It was the scribes and the Pharisees. They had elaborated and embellished the original Ten Commandments so much that they demanded that people tithe mint and cumin (a small herb and some seeds). Likewise, they insisted that even though one law claimed that people should honor their parents, an additional law stated that it was acceptable to take bread out of their parents' mouths and give it to the priests. Their convoluted twisting and bending of the law infuriated Jesus, a carpenter who only needed his heart, his head, and a simple ruler to measure things.

A proverb reads, "God confounds the wise and uplifts the simple." Often it is not the team with the biggest rule book, training manual, or business plan that wins; it is the one with the clearest concept. The first U.S. Army leadership manual, for example, summed up its principles into three key words: "Be, Know, and Do."

As a frequent traveler, I have had the pleasure and misfortune to encounter some of the best and worst service in the hospitality industry.

Last week I came upon a restaurant called the Bubba Gump Shrimp Company, located on the beautiful shores of Lahaina, Hawaii. Intrigued by the music and the decor, as well as by the friendly smiles of the people in the lobby, I went inside and sat down for lunch. On the table were two license plates, suspended on a flip-over device. One, in blue, read RUN FORREST RUN. The other, in red, said STOP FORREST STOP. As the hostess sat me down and handed me the menu, she said, "When everything is fine with you, leave the blue plate down. When you need anything at all, put up the red one." I tried it. The second I put up the red STOP FORREST STOP license plate, whoever was walking by would stop and ask how they could help me. It didn't matter who was assigned to my table, that employee took care of it. I had orders taken by busboys, questions on the establishment answered by waiters, and my table cleared by a manager. This team understood service, and had simplified a process so that customers were served when they needed attention, and left alone when they didn't. It was some of the finest service I'd ever encountered — all to background music of songs from the sixties.

When Jesus told the story about the good Samaritan defying tradition by touching an "enemy" who had fallen into a ditch, Jesus was saying "Keep it simple." When he told those surrounding the adulterous woman to throw the stones only if they were without sin, he was keeping it simple. When he told the disciples to feed the people who had gathered for a sermon, he was keeping it simple.

Some of the finest team service I have ever encountered had a training manual that consisted of six words: RUN FORREST RUN. STOP FORREST STOP.

Jesus said, "Unless you begin to think like a child, you cannot enter the kingdom of heaven." Jesus kept it simple.

Questions

1. What if you had to boil your team-training manual down into six words? What would those words be?
2. What organizations or institutions, in your experience, deliver some of the worst service in the world? What is the size of their training manuals?

> ## Prayer
>
> *Dear Lord,*
> *You said you came here to give us abundant life. Help me not*
> *to complicate things by trying to control them.*
>
> > *Amen*

HE DIDN'T YELL "COWARDS!"

AS THE CROWD DEPARTED

~

Father, forgive them, for they know not what they do.
— LUKE 23:34

BEING A TEAMBUILDER CAN be a lonely and isolating adventure. One of the truths about teambuilding is that just as you have to be prepared to scrape "Barnacle Bill and Betty" off your boat to keep it lean and clean, you also have to be prepared for the boat lurching in the water when former best friends and teammates "Edwina and Albert" jump ship and swim to shore in the middle of the night without saying good-bye. "Got a better offer" might read the note left on the coffee mug. "Couldn't take it anymore" might read the note on the refrigerator. "You have lost your mind! You're dangerous!" might read the note delivered by FedEx the next day, still billed on your account.

The fear of being abandoned is deeply ingrained in us. Even Jesus had an incredible need for companionship. Time and again he asked the disciples if they would wait with him, pray with him, walk with him, work with him. His greatest cry of agony on the cross was not because of the physical pain he was experiencing; it was the temporary abandonment that he felt. "My God, my God, why have you forsaken me?" he cried out, in the voice of an abandoned child.

So the truth is, it hurts when people leave us, no matter what the reason. "*Et tu, Brute?*" cried out Julius Caesar as Brutus, his former number-one fan and friend, plunged in the knife. Shakespeare found the theme of betrayal great fodder for his plays, because abandonment and betrayal are the stuff of human life.

So a team leader must not be surprised when the curtain rises and suddenly half the cast is gone. David Gergen, former consultant to presidents Reagan, Bush, and Clinton, said he was amazed at how often the feeling that "if I call, no one will answer" plagued even the most powerful, because "success has many fathers, but failure only one." When times got tough it was amazing to them how many former friends suddenly disappeared.

That is why it is imperative that you are clear about your personal mission, and that you always remember that the human heart is fickle.

You have been called into this leadership position, no matter what it is, because Someone had faith that when the smoke from the battle cleared, you would still be in your assigned post no matter what the others did.

Joseph was sold into slavery by his jealous brothers, but lived to serve them in a larger capacity, saying "God meant it for good."

Jesus did not utter a word of condemnation against those who abandoned him in his darkest hour. Instead he said, "Father, forgive them, for they know not what they do." There was no desire for revenge, perhaps because he knew that no matter what, he was going home.

Jesus did not yell "Cowards!" when the crowds departed.

Questions

1. Would you be shocked, saddened, dismayed, and bitter if the people closest to you turned tail and ran?
2. Would you let their actions define your agenda?
3. Do you take every resignation personally?
4. Did Jesus?

Prayer

Dear Lord,
Help me realize the hard truth that even after I pour everything I am into this team, some of them might leave, and others might betray me. Let me continue to love them anyway, knowing that you are my Source, and that only you are True.

Amen

HE KNEW THERE WAS A LITTLE BIT OF CRAZY IN ALL OF US

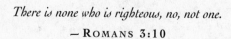

There is none who is righteous, no, not one.
— ROMANS 3:10

TEAM LEADERS WILL DO well to quickly rid themselves of the notion that their team consists of normal people. You will recognize, over time, that even the most "normal" among us are beset by fears, failings, childhood traumas, feelings of inadequacy, or other dark clouds. You never can tell just by looking at someone on the surface what his or her heart holds inside.

I have a dear friend named Bonnie Dawson, who, with her partner and coworker, George Hester, work with financial planning needs for very wealthy families — specializing in people with earnings of $3 million or more. What George has discovered, and brought Bonnie in to help with, is that planning a family's financial future brings up a host of buried issues totally unrelated to the money on the table. Bonnie is a licensed family and marriage counselor who goes in with George and watches transactions that are taking place, then advises him where the cracks in the family's true foundation are. Then they lovingly, and with permission only, begin to address the real needs. I have heard tales (no client names included) of distant fathers being undermined by resentful children, wives in the throes of depression contemplating suicide, all dressed in the finest clothes and living in beautiful mansions. As Bonnie told me one day, "Laurie Beth, there is a nickel's worth of crazy in all of us — so I am never surprised by what turns up."

In the book *A Shepherd Looks at the 23rd Psalm*, the author, Phillip Keller, who tended sheep for his family business in Africa, discusses the duties of a good shepherd. He writes that because sheeps' wool can hide a multitude of scratches, cuts, and parasites, the shepherd's duty at the beginning and end of each day is to carefully and lovingly examine each sheep to make sure that there is no hidden wound that might later become infected. He writes that only careless shepherds just turn their animals out to graze without daily inspections, and they usually suffer for it when the animals get sick, drop weight, or injure themselves.

Jesus was able to sense the wounded craziness in each of the people he encountered. He saw it in Peter's erratic attempts to please. He saw it in the woman with five husbands, or the woman caught in adultery, or the man possessed by a legion of demons. He was not put off by these things, but moved by them — into these people's hearts, so that he could make a difference.

Quite often, irrational or unacceptable behavior by one of your team members means that he or she is reacting not to the current situation, but to something not dealt with in his or her personal life.

Am I saying that good team leaders all need to become therapists? No. Good team leaders learn to recognize that all of us have hidden issues that may be driving us, for ill or for good, and they are willing to take the time to help identify the problem, and deal with it, or refer us to others who can.

I recently conducted a seminar where one gentleman persistently talked during the presentations, despite my best efforts to shush him. At the break, his supervisor came up to me and said, "That's just Steve. Don't take it personally. We think he has

ADD—but he's been with us seventeen years and is a great worker in the warehouse, so we put up with his jabbering." This supervisor was demonstrating his awareness of a little bit of craziness in an employee that had been lovingly accommodated for by him and the other members of the team.

Jesus was able to say, "I know my own, and my own know me."

Uncomfortable and time-consuming as the task of checking the sheep daily for wounds might be, it will definitely make for a healthier and more trusting flock.

Jesus looked for where the hurt was, and he addressed it.

Jesus knew there was a little bit of crazy in all of us.

Questions

1. Are you assuming that all of your team members are "normal"?
2. What is the danger in that kind of thinking?
3. How aware are you of your people's issues and deep needs?
4. How are you addressing those needs?
5. What could be the benefits of being aware of the "little bit of crazy" in all people?

Prayer

Dear Lord,
You certainly know that there is a little bit of craziness in me.
Take your hand and heal me, and help me learn to look out,
like a good shepherd, for the cuts and parasites under the wool
of my flock.

Amen

HE MADE THEM FEEL WELCOME

"And when his father saw him, he ran to meet him."

— LUKE 15:20

THE MORE I DEAL with people in transition, the more aware I become that one of their root issues is never having felt welcome, not only in organizations or families or teams, but sometimes in the world itself.

Last week I stood before a group of thirty-five business and community leaders, all dressed in the casual attire the resort location inspired. Earlier that evening we had laughed and clinked glasses together in joy at the prospects of this retreat. About five hours into the workshop I introduced the "Cup of Sorrow," which is used in our Path Training workshops.

In this particular exercise I ask people to identify the ingredients in the cup of sorrow that both their mother and father were drinking from.

One woman, a sharply dressed, articulate, confident sales trainer, shared that her mother never wanted her, that in fact it was her father's intervention that prevented her from being aborted. Hence her mother's cup of sorrow was filled with blame, bitterness, and regret, and her father's cup was filled with a longing to have had a loving wife and a happy family.

As we role-played the conversations between this woman, whom I'll call Susan, and her mother, I asked a gentleman from the back to come forward and intercede. "Michael, will you be Jesus?" I asked. "When Susan's mother tries to give her the cup of sorrow she's drinking, you step between them, take it, drink it, and then turn it over so that Susan can see the last drop dripping to the floor." He did so, saying to Susan, "Susan, I was there for your mother when she conceived you, and I have been with her every day of her life. I am taking and drinking her cup of sorrow so that you will no longer have to." With that, he took the cup and drank it, then turned it upside down.

As the last few drops from the cup hit the floor, Susan collapsed crying into Michael's (Jesus') arms. Standing before the three of them—mother, Jesus, and Susan—I could see that many of the rest of the group were weeping, a few out loud.

When I walked over to the woman who was sobbing most loudly, she gasped out, "I was supposed to have been aborted, too." Blessedly, I had with me a professionally trained therapist, and as we began to walk up quietly to the people who were weeping, the floodgates opened.

Another woman had been the victim of a stepfather's sexual abuse. Her mother had known about it but had never intervened.

A man said his father never made him feel welcome at all, or showed him any approval. All he said was "You could have done better," or "Why aren't you doing more?"

You would never have known by looking at this previously laughing, affluent group of executives and entrepreneurs that their hearts had been wounded by feeling unwelcome in their own families of origin. Many of them were preparing to leave work situations because they felt unwanted there, too.

Yesterday I sat with a woman who expressed concerns about

her ten-year-old daughter's behavior. "She never wants to come out of her room," she complained. "She's even built a tent over her bed—where she eats and reads and calls her friends. She's not outgoing like her three older brothers, and she rarely expresses affection, especially to me."

It was later that her mother confessed that she had initially planned to abort the child. Both she and her husband had felt they had their hands full and were concerned about the demands that a "late" child would bring. "Ultimately, we decided to keep her, and I'm glad we did," said the mother. "Yet sometimes I worry about her being so withdrawn."

I couldn't help but flash back to the group I had been with only a short while before. Perhaps the child had heard her parents' discussions even while in the womb. Perhaps that is why she wants only to remain in her room, a tent pulled safely over her head.

The need for welcome cannot be overestimated—at any age, at any level of interaction between human beings.

Craig Tysdale, the CEO of NetSolve, insists on personally conducting the orientation of all new hires, wanting them to see from him how really welcome they are.

Does your team feel welcomed and wanted by you? Do its members make others feel welcomed, as well? The essence of teambuilding is connection, and the simplest and most profound connections begin when someone says, "Hi. I'm so glad you're here."

When Jesus said "I go to prepare a place for you," he was intending to show them, upon their arrival, just how really excited and welcome they were. When he spoke about the angels in heaven rejoicing whenever a single soul turns home, he was again demonstrating the importance of welcome.

Jesus made them feel welcome.

Questions

1. Do you make your teammates feel welcomed? How?
2. Who has made you feel most welcomed in recent memory? How did they do so?
3. What was the result?
4. How can you ensure that a culture of welcome exists for your team?
5. What could be the result?

Prayer

Dear Lord,
You made me feel welcomed into your family through the invitation of your very own son. Help me demonstrate your sense of welcome to everyone I meet and especially to those on my team and in my family.

Amen

HE LED THEM TO FACE
THEIR UNFACEABLES

The people that sat in darkness have seen a great light.
— MATTHEW 4:16

A S I WATCHED THE workers smoothing the newly poured concrete for the patio, I found great visual satisfaction in the
trowels moving methodically and rapidly over the shimmering
surface. I could just picture myself sitting there in the evening,
enjoying the sunset as I stepped out from the newly installed
French doors. Leaving the workers to their work, I went about
doing mine.

I took no notice of the trees growing all around. Eight months
later I was standing not on a smooth patio, but one with fractures
all through it and a huge crack down the middle.

"I didn't know El Paso had earthquakes," I said disappointedly
to the person now standing beside me, surveying the damage. "It
doesn't," said he, adjusting his baseball cap. "Your contractor
failed to account for the roots underground." Slowly the truth
sank in — I couldn't fix this crack by simply pouring more cement
into it. The whole area had to be dug up.

Peter was the first of the disciples to recognize that Jesus was indeed the Messiah. Peter proved loyal and ferocious in his deeds and actions—always being the first off the boat. Jesus could easily have promoted him to the top of the list, which he later did. However, there was a root problem that Peter needed to face before he could move up. "Peter, I tell you that before this day is over, you will deny me three times."

Jesus was making Peter face his unfaceable issue, which was the need for human approval. Notice that he never withdrew his love and support during these positive confrontations. He conveyed in his manner and bearing that the unpleasant issue was not going to cause him to draw away—yet *they* could not move forward until they recognized and faced the problems.

I sat in the expansive boardroom overlooking the beautiful lakes and fields of the Las Colinas development. Doug Hawthorne, the CEO of Texas Health Resources, had invited me to come help, in his words "save the soul of the organization," a massive healthcare entity with fifteen thousand employees. The organization had just completed two mergers and was facing another one. Doug felt that his most important charge was to ensure that the spiritual heart and mission of their work be kept in constant focus during the challenging times ahead. As a person who has seen Doug in action over a four-year period, I can tell you that Doug's core value is relationships.

Today Doug's usually smiling face was serious. He was sharing with me one of the major initiatives the board had decided to allocate millions of dollars to address: domestic violence. He sighed as he began. "Laurie Beth, as you know, our mission is to improve the health of the communities we serve. We commissioned studies to determine what were some core community health issues we should address. Guess what we discovered. Our emergency rooms were being filled not with gang-related shootings, but with battered wives. A bruise here, a broken shoulder there, multiple stab wounds in the face. We then studied charts brought in by our physicians. We enlisted the police to share their crime reports. And we realized that we were not dealing with a few isolated incidents, but with a hidden epidemic — one that is not restricted to lower-income neighborhoods or minorities, but one that has infected every level and income group in our community. We then looked at absentee statistics from major employers, which confirmed to us that this problem of domestic violence has a devastating effect socially, physically, spiritually, and economically.

"When we compared our community statistics with national statistics, we realized to our horror that we were not the exception, but were typical of domestic assault figures in this country.

"We extrapolated the averages, and had to face the fact that among our own fifteen thousand employees, 80 percent of whom are women, we have at least one thousand — probably more like three thousand — of our own staff members being battered by their domestic partners."

Then he fell silent. He stood up and walked over to the window, his hands deep in his pockets. Doug and his organization were about to launch a major initiative to face the unfaceable — especially among their own. This initiative included massive community training programs, as well as simply placing employee hotline numbers in restrooms. (For more information on the Texas Health Resources Family Violence Prevention Initiative, call 817-462-7073.)

This incredible organization was about to go into a new kind of "heart care," if you will — all because the leadership realized that you couldn't cement over deep-rooted problems just by putting a big, fancy plaque with a spiritual message statement on your wall.

Jesus had them face the unfaceables.

Questions

1. What issues have you been unwilling to face, in yourself, in your team, and in your individual team members?
2. What is it costing you not to face those issues?
3. How long do you plan to enjoy your patio?

> ## Prayer
>
> *Dear Lord,*
> *You said the truth will make us free. Help us be willing to face the unfaceable, so that then your face may shine.*
> *Amen*

He Made Training
the Reward

*"The words I have spoken to you are spirit
and they are life."*
— John 6:63

In their book *Values Shift*, John Izzo and Pam Withers reveal that the one thing the new worker wants almost more than money is training. With corporate ladders disappearing and organizations flattening out, people are realizing that in order to stay current and competitive, they constantly need to be learning new skills that will keep them flexible — and stimulated — as they move through work.

Jesus promised his workers new information and new skills on a never-ending basis. "There are other things I have yet to tell you," he said, letting them know that their training would be ongoing. "Those who are faithful with little will be given more." That is, once you've mastered certain skills, we will entrust you with new tasks and even more training. "I will make you fishers of men." By which he meant, "I will take the skills you now have, and train you so that your mastery is expanded beyond even your current industry."

Sears has a career development program that ensures that its information technicians enjoy varied work assignments, as well as career training and advice. Companies such as Sun Micro-Systems, Microsoft, and Procter & Gamble do the same.

I recently spoke at Adventist Health Care, a hospital that is part of a worldwide health-care system, at a meeting for their human resources departments. The leadership team has instilled and nurtured a corporate culture that encourages people to "look beyond your desks—beyond your ivory tower, and get out there and learn something new—preferably in the fields." They have cross-functional team meetings to identify the new opportunities and challenges each department is facing. If someone in another department wants to take on the problem, leaders give that person the chance to do field research and on-the-job training to help identify solutions.

Earlier I had spoken to Tom, a man who has been with the system for twenty-eight years. When I asked him why he had stayed so long, he said, "Because there is always something new to learn around here! I have never been bored!"

Jesus never had a recruitment problem. He promised to enroll his team in God's university of never-ending learning and spiritual thrills. Who wouldn't want to work in such a place?

Jesus made training a reward.

Questions

1. How much new training do you offer your team?
2. What do your training classes look like? Boring or open-ended?
3. Why do you think Jesus offered training, rather than golden harps, as the reward?
4. What are you learning that's new?

He Shared Responsibility
for Customer Satisfaction

Phillip, how shall we feed these people?
— John 6:5

IN THEIR BOOK *Digital Capital: Harnessing the Power of the Business Web*, authors Don Tapscot, David Ticoll, and Alex Lowy attempt to nail down the esoteric differences that make companies like Cisco Systems grow so fast and operate so efficiently. One of the keys they discovered was that "Cisco owns only two of the thirty-eight plants that assemble its products, and operates with a mindset of shared responsibility for customer satisfaction." In other words, every person and organization in its business web is *fully*, not *partially*, responsible for excellence and service.

Like it or not, this seems to be the business model and team organizational chart that Jesus set up: "Whatever you do to them, you do to me" (Matthew 25:40); "If anyone gives you even a cup of water in my name, they will receive a prophet's reward" (Matthew 10:42).

The famous story of the Good Samaritan was in essence a reflection of the new corporate team-building philosophy. A man was beaten by robbers and thrown into a ditch (not the team's fault). Several people pass by, and see him, including designated team leaders (scribes and Pharisees). They look down at him and say, "Not our job."

The Samaritan, however, a person not on the team, comes along and decides to take responsibility for this customer in need. In fact, he goes well beyond what most of us would have done, giving a blank check to cover the man's expenses.

"Ah, this is teamwork," says Jesus. "If you see the problem, you own it," reads the Ritz-Carlton Hotel training manual.

When Allegiance Healthcare in El Paso, Texas, gave production workers responsibility for making assembly-line purchasing and shipping decisions that had formerly been left to supervisors, sales per employee rose 61 percent.

During a recent spring cleaning, a neighborhood resident placed certain items in the alley for subsequent pickup by a local charity group called Candlelighters. Included among the items was an old, rusty bicycle with flat tires and a broken seat. The bicycle quickly disappeared, and it was assumed that someone had stolen it. A day later the bicycle reappeared in the same spot — cleaned, oiled, and with the tires and seat fixed. Like the Good Samaritan praised by Jesus, this anonymous neighbor saw an opportunity for service, and took it.

Jesus shared responsibility for customer satisfaction.

Questions

1. What aspect of the work that your team does, particularly as it relates to people, is "not your job"?
2. Does anyone on your team exhibit a "not my job" mentality?
3. Does a lack of "ownership" in your team's duties reflect itself in a lack of "stewardship"?
4. How would your team's performance improve if there was a sense of "shared responsibility for customer satisfaction?"

EPILOGUE

A RECENT ARTICLE ON artificial intelligence stated that although experts predict that they can create a computer to think like a human within the next four years, it will take an additional forty-four years of sophisticated programming before they can teach a computer to think like a *team*.

As a teambuilder, you have been given perhaps the most challenging and rewarding work on the planet today, which is teaching human beings to think and act like a team.

In *Teach Your Team to Fish*, you have been given more than fifty tips on teambuilding, such as how to make everyone feel welcome and wanted, how to encourage them to face their unfaceables, how to teach them to choose their battles, and how to turn everyone into a recruiter.

You also now know that in order to teach your team to fish you must

Excite Them,

Ground Them,

Transform Them, and

Release Them.

I pray that the insights you have received while reading this book, which is based on the life of the greatest Fisherman and Teambuilder of all time, have assisted you on your way.

I also pray that after your work is done, you can pray, as Jesus did, "They were your gifts, and you gave them to me. . . . I pray also that they may be One, even as you and I are One."

My prayers are for you, and the Oneness of your team.

LAURIE BETH JONES

ACKNOWLEDGMENTS

I have been blessed with an incredibly diverse and talented team in putting this book (and my life) together. I want especially to thank Catherine Calhoun, who introduced me to systems thinking. The dynamic team who assists me every day includes Rosario Muñoz, Marty Blubaugh, Robin Chaddock, Terry Barber, Eric Boutieller, Kati Gerdau, and Bill Jackson. Crown Business has gifted me with the talents of Ruth Mills and John Mahaney, my never-give-up editors, Shana Wingert, and the promotional team of Will Weisser and Darlene Faster. Kim Garrison of CLASS public relations also helped move the books off the shelves. My agent, Mary Ann Naples, helped pave the way for the spirituality-in-business movement through her early recognition of the truth that was happening and became an early advocate of the movement through championing *Jesus, CEO*.

Associates who particularly blessed me this year include Ken and Margie Blanchard, Mike Regan, Dick Stenbakken, Greg Bunch, Bob Hertel, Tom Addington, Steve Graves, Bob Buford, Phil Hodges, Larry Spears, Robin Wood, Carlin Johnson, Tom Heck, Kim Clegg, Jim and Terry Ellick, Janet Ellis, James T. Harris, Charley Waldo, Claudia Coe, Sally Young, Ginny Ogden, Betty Ann Bird, Lisa Dahlberg, Dee and Adair Margo, Terry and Renee Hornbuckle, Linda Sterrett Marple, Roger Danforth, Ed Blitz, Dave Cowan, Susanna Palomares, Katherine Kellison McLaughlin, Nicole Johnson, JannaLee Sponberg, and Kathy Marcil.

To my family as always, thank you for loving me: my incredible mother, Irene Jones; Kathy, Ben, Bennie, Wade, and Tara Ivey;

Joe Jones and Barbara Hanlon; Irma Soto; Ricardo and Irene, and Joseph and Jacob Prat; Yvonne and Miguel, and Gabriel and Antonio Gomez; and Joshua, Chula, Sunny, and Little Pistol. Each of you helps remind me what life is all about through your unbridled joy.

To my Love, Jesus, thank you for once again allowing me to write about You.

INDEX

About the Author

LAURIE BETH JONES is the author of the national bestsellers *Jesus, CEO; Jesus in Blue Jeans;* and *The Path,* as well as *Jesus, Inc; The Power of Positive Prophecy;* and *Grow Something Besides Old.* She is also a nationally acclaimed author and speaker, whose work has been heralded and discussed from the halls of the Pentagon to the streets of Calcutta, being translated into twelve foreign languages. As a consultant, she conducts seminars worldwide on leadership, on teambuilding, and on mission and vision. She also consults one-on-one with CEOs and leadership teams and trains facilitators to help coach their organizations, departments, and groups. She lives in West Texas. For more information, visit her website at www.jesusceo.com.

Laurie Beth Jones is available for the following:

- speaking at your event
- consulting with your organization on leadership and team-building
- conducting customized leadership retreats
- conducting customized Vision Quests

To learn about how to become a trained Path facilitator, sign up for the Jesus, CEO online courses and receive our free e-mail updates, contact us at www.jesusceo.com, or e-mail us at ljones@elp.rr.com. We can be reached by phone at (915) 541-6033 or fax (915) 541-6034. (For information on How to Write Your Book, including agent contact numbers, log on to our website.)

To learn more about WaterBrook Press and view
our catalog of products, log on to our Web site:
www.waterbrookpress.com

WATERBROOK
PRESS